I0454170

LLC Beginner's Guide

Master Business with the Ultimate Guide to Forming, Managing, and Growing Your Limited Liability Company - Realize Your Vision with Expert Insights and Proven Strategies.

Arnold Kent Tyler

In the final pages of this book will give you instant access to the two bonuses you have been promised:

1. the introductory video
2. the complete audio guide covering the entire book.

....

"An investment in education pays the best interest."

Benjamin Franklin.

Table of Contents

Introduction

Hello everyone! If you're thinking of starting your own business and have heard about LLCs, or "Limited Liability Companies," but are unsure about what you should do, you're in the right place. This guide will explain, step by step, in simple and comprehensive terms, everything you need to know about LLCs, how to form them, and how to keep them operational. Most importantly, it will cover the differences between LLCs and other corporate forms and why you should choose an LLC. Don't worry, I've made it super easy to understand!

Moreover, as the author of this manual, I make you a promise: to take you from where you are now to where you want to be. This guide will serve as your compass, pointing you in the right direction both on good days and in the challenging times you may encounter. Each section is crafted with practical examples that simplify understanding, making each concept clear and accessible, one topic at a time.

My heart and experience are poured into these pages, creating a guide that transcends the dryness of a textbook and embraces the warmth of a conversation with a mentor who has already navigated these waters. This journey is much more than just imparting knowledge; it's about empowering you to start and continue with a solid foundation and a clear direction. This is my vow to help you achieve mastery and success.

Notices:

- The company names used as examples are fictional; any real-world relevance is purely coincidental.

- All registered trademarks mentioned in the book belong to their rightful owners.

- Please refer to the legal disclaimer at the end of this book for important information on the content provided.

Decoding LLCs: Your FAQ Resource

How do you form an LLC?

To form an LLC, you must choose a unique name for your company, appoint a registered agent, file the Articles of Organization with your state, and create an operating agreement that outlines the management and operations of your LLC.

How many members are needed to form an LLC?

An LLC can be formed by a single member (single-member LLC) or multiple members. There is no maximum limit to the number of members.

How much does it cost to form an LLC?

Costs vary depending on the state in which the LLC is formed. Generally, there are filing fees for the Articles of Organization and there may be annual costs for reports and licenses.

Does an LLC have to pay income taxes on business earnings?

Typically, LLCs are considered pass-through entities for tax purposes, meaning earnings pass through to the members who then report them on their personal tax returns. However, an LLC can choose to be taxed as a corporation.

What are the main documents required to manage an LLC?

The main documents include the Articles of Organization, the operating agreement, and, in many states, an annual report. Industry-specific licenses and permits may also be necessary.

How do you protect the limited liability of an LLC?

To maintain the protection of limited liability, it is important to keep personal finances separate from business finances, adhere to all legal formalities such as holding regular meetings and recording business decisions, and ensure compliance with all applicable laws and regulations.

Can I convert my existing business into an LLC?

Yes, many businesses can convert their existing structure into an LLC, but the process varies by state and type of current business structure. It is advisable to consult a lawyer or tax advisor to understand the process and implications.

Can an LLC have employees?

Yes, an LLC can hire employees. It must comply with all applicable employment laws, including registering for payroll taxes and workers' compensation insurance.

How do you dissolve an LLC?

To dissolve an LLC, members generally need to vote for dissolution and then file the Articles of Dissolution with the state. Afterwards, it is necessary to liquidate the business assets, pay off debts, and distribute any remaining assets to the members.

Can I form an LLC in a different state from where I live?

Yes, you can form an LLC in a different state from where you reside. However, you will need to appoint a registered agent in that state and may face additional requirements and taxes.

What is the difference between a member and a manager in an LLC?

A member is an owner of an LLC. An LLC can be managed by members (member-managed) or can appoint one or more managers (manager-managed) to handle day-to-day operations.

Can an LLC issue stock?

No, LLCs do not issue stock. Ownership of an LLC is defined through membership interests, as outlined in the operating agreement.

How do you transfer ownership of an LLC?

Transferring ownership of an LLC can be complex and is usually governed by the operating agreement. It may require the consent of other members and, in some cases, adherence to specific state laws.

Can an LLC have investors?

Yes, an LLC can have investors. Investors can become

members of the LLC or may participate in other ways, depending on the operating agreement and applicable laws.

How do you pay yourself from an LLC?

Members of an LLC typically receive payments through direct withdrawals from the LLC's profits (distributions) or, if the LLC opts to be taxed as a corporation, through a regular salary.

Can an LLC be publicly traded?

No, LLCs usually cannot be publicly traded. Companies that wish to go public typically organize as corporations.

What are the differences between an LLC and an S-Corp or a C-Corp?

LLCs are generally more flexible and have fewer formal requirements compared to S-Corps and C-Corps. S-Corps and C-Corps can issue stock and are subject to stricter rules. S-Corps have limitations on the number and type of shareholders, while C-Corps are subject to double taxation on profits.

Do I need to renew my LLC every year?

Many states require LLCs to file an annual report and pay an annual or periodic fee. Specific requirements vary from state to state.

What happens if an LLC member dies or decides to leave the company?

The operating agreement should outline the process for handling the departure or death of a member. Without an operating agreement specifying otherwise, state laws usually provide for the dissolution of the LLC unless the remaining members decide to continue the business.

Exploring the Chapters: a Snapshot

An LLC is like a special box where you can put your business. This box protects your personal stuff (like your house and car) if your business runs into trouble, like debts or lawsuits. It's a popular way to start a business in the United States because it's flexible and not too complicated.

Chapter 2: Setting Up Your LLC

First things first, you need to pick a unique name for your LLC that no other business is using. Then, you need to find someone who can receive important papers for your business; this person is called a "registered agent." Lastly, you need to fill out a special paper called "Articles of Organization" and send it to your state government with a small fee.

Chapter 3: Running Your LLC

Now that you have your LLC, how do you run it? Well, you can decide if you and the other owners want to manage it together or if you want to hire someone to do it. It's also a good idea to write down rules about how to make decisions and split the money; these rules are called an "Operating Agreement."

Chapter 4: Taxes and Money

One great thing about LLCs is that you don't have to pay extra taxes. The money earned or lost by your business goes straight to you and other owners, and you report it on your personal taxes. Sometimes, though, it might be better for your LLC to pay taxes like it's a big company. This is a choice you can make.

Chapter 5: Keeping Your LLC in Good Standing

Every year, you need to tell your state how your LLC is doing. This usually means filling out a simple form and paying a fee. It's like an annual check-up for your business.

Chapter 6: If You Decide to Close

If one day you decide you don't want your LLC anymore, there's a right way to close it. You need to make sure to pay off all debts, sell off your business stuff, and tell your state that you're shutting down.

Conclusion:

There you have it! Now you know the basics of LLCs. They're a great way to protect yourself while doing business. Remember, each state has slightly different rules, so it's always a good idea to talk to an expert if you have specific questions. Good luck with your business!

1. Chapter 1: What's an LLC?

Welcome to the first step of your entrepreneurial journey! Understanding what an LLC is will lay the foundation for your business's future. So, let's dive in!

Sec. 1.1: The Basics of an LLC – With Comparative Examples

An LLC, or Limited Liability Company, is a type of business structure that's unique to the United States. It combines the simplicity of a sole proprietorship or partnership with the liability protection of a corporation. Think of it as a hybrid with the best of both worlds.

An LLC is a popular business structure in the United States, known for its flexibility and protection. To truly understand its unique position, let's compare it with other common types of business entities: sole proprietorships, partnerships, and corporations.

Sole Proprietorship:

A sole proprietorship is the simplest business form, where one individual owns and operates the business. There's no legal distinction between the owner and the business.

Example: Jane's Catering Service is owned and run solely by Jane. She's responsible for all debts and liabilities. As a sole proprietor, Jane enjoys full control over her business decisions and receives all the profits. However, this business structure does not offer any separation between her personal and business assets. Here's how this lack of separation can impact her.

Personal Liability for Business Debts:

If Jane's Catering Service incurs debts, such as unpaid supplier bills or a business loan, creditors can pursue Jane's personal assets to recover the debts. This means her personal savings, car, or even her home could be at risk if her business cannot pay its debts.

Example: Jane takes out a loan to expand her catering kitchen. If the business fails to generate enough revenue to repay the loan, the lender can go after Jane's personal bank accounts or property.

Personal Liability for Legal Actions:

In a sole proprietorship, the owner is personally liable for any legal actions taken against the business. If Jane's Catering Service is sued for any reason, such as a customer falling ill due to food poisoning, Jane is personally responsible. Any legal settlements or judgments could come out of her personal assets.

Example: A customer contracts food poisoning at an event catered by Jane's service and decides to sue. If the court rules in favor of the customer, Jane may have to pay the settlement from her personal funds.

Mixing Personal and Business Finances:

Many sole proprietors, especially in the early stages, mix their personal and business finances. This can complicate tax filings and make it difficult to track the business's financial performance. Moreover, it reinforces the lack of separation between personal and business assets.

Example: Jane uses her personal credit card to purchase supplies for her catering business and also uses the business's revenue to pay for her personal expenses. This commingling of funds can lead to financial disorganization and potential legal issues.

Conclusion:

In Jane's Catering Service, as a sole proprietorship, there's no legal distinction between Jane and her business. While this structure is simple and straightforward, it exposes Jane's personal assets to significant risk. This example underscores the importance of understanding the implications of different business structures and choosing one that aligns with your risk tolerance and business needs.

Partnership:

A partnership is similar to a sole proprietorship but involves two or more people. Partners share profits, losses, and management responsibilities.

Example: Smith & Wesson Law Firm is owned by John Smith and Jane Wesson. They share profits and are jointly responsible for the firm's liabilities. In a partnership, both partners share profits, management responsibilities, and liabilities. Here's how their personal assets can be involved:

Joint and Several Liability:

In a general partnership, both partners are jointly and severally liable for the actions of the partnership. This means that if the firm incurs debts or is sued, both John and Jane can be held personally responsible, even for actions taken by the other partner.

Example: If John enters into a contract with a vendor for office supplies and the firm fails to pay, the vendor can seek payment from either John or Jane's personal assets, not just the business assets.

Shared Responsibility for Legal Actions:

If Smith & Wesson Law Firm is sued for malpractice, both John and Jane are personally liable. This means that their personal assets, such as homes, cars, and savings, could be used to settle any legal claims.

Example: A client sues the firm for malpractice, alleging that poor legal advice led to financial loss. If the court rules against the firm, both John and Jane's personal assets could be at risk to cover the damages.

Personal Guarantees for Business Loans:

Partners often have to provide personal guarantees to secure business loans. This means that if the business cannot repay the loan, the partners are personally responsible for the debt.

Example: Smith & Wesson Law Firm takes out a loan to expand their office. Both John and Jane sign personal guarantees. If the firm cannot make the loan payments, the bank can go after both partners' personal assets.

Dissolution and Debts:

If the partnership dissolves, both partners are responsible for any remaining business debts. This can lead to complex situations, especially if one partner is unable or unwilling to contribute to settling the debts.

Example: If John and Jane decide to dissolve the partnership but have outstanding business debts, they both are responsible for paying off those debts. If Jane cannot afford her share, creditors may pursue John's personal assets for the full amount.

Conclusion:

In the Smith & Wesson Law Firm partnership, both John and Jane's personal assets are intertwined with the business's liabilities. While partnerships allow for shared management and profits, they also come with shared risks. This example highlights the importance of carefully considering the implications of a partnership structure and taking steps to mitigate personal liability risks.

Corporation:

A corporation is a separate legal entity owned by shareholders. It offers strong liability protection but is more complex and subject to double taxation (the corporation and the shareholders are taxed separately).

Example: TechGiant Inc. is owned by multiple shareholders. It's taxed on its profits, and shareholders are also taxed on their dividends. A corporation is a separate legal entity, providing a clear distinction between the company and its owners. Here's how this structure impacts the involvement of personal assets:

Limited Liability Protection:

Shareholders of TechGiant Inc. enjoy limited liability protection. This means their personal assets are generally not at risk for the debts and liabilities of the corporation. Shareholders' losses are limited to the amount they invested in the company.

Example: If TechGiant Inc. is sued for a defective product, the shareholders are not personally liable. Their risk is limited to their investment in the company's stock, and their personal assets, such as homes or savings, are protected.

No Personal Responsibility for Corporate Debts:

Shareholders are not personally responsible for the corporation's debts. If TechGiant Inc. takes out a loan and defaults, the creditors cannot go after the shareholders' personal assets.

Example: TechGiant Inc. fails to repay a substantial business loan. The bank can seize the company's assets, but it cannot touch the personal assets of the shareholders.

Separation of Personal and Business Finances:

Corporations require a clear separation of personal and business finances. Shareholders do not use their personal accounts for business transactions, and the corporation has its own credit and financial standing.

Example: A shareholder of TechGiant Inc. cannot use the company's funds to pay for personal expenses without proper authorization and documentation. Doing so could breach the corporate veil and potentially expose personal assets to risk.

Personal Guarantees and Director Liability:

While shareholders generally have limited liability, there are exceptions. If a shareholder (often in the case of small, closely-held corporations) provides a personal guarantee for a loan or is involved in wrongful acts as a director or officer, they could be held personally liable.

Example: If a shareholder of TechGiant Inc. personally guarantees a business loan, they are responsible for repaying the loan if the corporation defaults. Additionally, if a shareholder-director engages in fraudulent activities, they could be personally liable for the consequences.

Conclusion:

In TechGiant Inc., the corporate structure provides shareholders with significant protection of their personal assets. The clear legal separation between the corporation and its owners safeguards personal assets from the company's liabilities and debts. This example underscores the benefits of the corporate structure in terms of personal asset protection, though it also highlights the importance of maintaining proper corporate formalities to preserve this protection.

LLC (Limited Liability Company):

Let's get to the heart of the matter. We're sorry for spending time on other corporate forms in a simple way, but it was necessary for you to fully grasp the advantages of an LLC.

An LLC combines elements of sole proprietorships, partnerships, and corporations. Like a corporation, it offers liability protection, meaning the owners' personal assets are generally protected from business debts and lawsuits. Like sole proprietorships and partnerships, it can have a flexible management structure and benefits from pass-through taxation (avoiding double taxation).

Example: GreenThumb Gardens LLC is owned by three members. They enjoy liability protection, meaning their personal assets are safe if the business incurs debt. Profits and losses pass through to their personal tax returns, avoiding double taxation.

An LLC is designed to provide its members with liability protection while allowing for flexible management and taxation. Here's how this structure impacts the involvement of personal assets.

Limited Liability Protection:

The members of GreenThumb Gardens LLC enjoy limited liability protection, meaning their personal assets are generally shielded from the business's debts and legal liabilities. Members are only at risk for the amount they've invested in the LLC.

Example: If GreenThumb Gardens LLC faces a lawsuit for a landscaping mishap, the members' personal assets, such as their homes, cars, or personal bank accounts, are typically not at risk. Creditors can pursue the LLC's assets, but not the personal assets of the members.

Separation of Personal and Business Finances:

To maintain limited liability protection, it's crucial for the members to keep a clear separation between their personal and business finances. This means not using personal accounts for business transactions and vice versa.

Example: A member of GreenThumb Gardens LLC should not use the LLC's bank account to pay for personal expenses like a family vacation. Doing so could breach the "corporate veil" and potentially expose personal assets to risk.

Personal Guarantees and Member Actions:

While the LLC structure provides liability protection, there are exceptions. If a member provides a personal guarantee for a business loan or engages in wrongful acts, they could be held personally liable.

Example: If a member personally guarantees a loan for GreenThumb Gardens LLC and the LLC defaults, the member is personally responsible for repaying the loan. Additionally, if a member commits fraud or negligence in the course of business, they could be personally liable for the consequences.

Conclusion:

In GreenThumb Gardens LLC, the LLC structure provides members with significant protection of their personal assets from the company's liabilities and debts. However, this protection is contingent on maintaining proper separation between personal and business finances and avoiding personal guarantees or wrongful actions. This example highlights the benefits of the LLC structure in terms of personal asset protection, as well as the responsibilities members have to maintain that protection.

Key Differences:

Liability: Sole proprietors and partners have unlimited personal liability for business debts, while LLC members and corporate shareholders enjoy liability protection.

Taxation: Sole proprietorships and partnerships have pass-through taxation. Corporations face double taxation unless they elect S-Corp status. LLCs have the default benefit of pass-through taxation with the option to be taxed as a corporation if beneficial.

Complexity: Sole proprietorships and partnerships are simpler to form and operate. Corporations require more formalities, like issuing stock and holding board meetings. LLCs strike a balance, offering protection and flexibility with fewer formalities than corporations.

Conclusion:

Understanding the basics of an LLC and how it compares to other business entities can help you make an informed decision about the right structure for your business. Each has its advantages and considerations, and the best choice depends on your specific business needs, goals, and risk tolerance.

Sec. 1.2: Liability Protection

One of the biggest perks of an LLC is right in its name: limited liability. This means if your business faces debts or legal issues, your personal assets (like your home, car, or personal bank accounts) are usually safe. You're not personally on the hook for the business's liabilities, which provides a safety net as you venture into the business world. This section will delve into what liability protection means, how it works, and its limitations.

Understanding Limited Liability:

The principle of limited liability provides that the personal assets of LLC members are generally protected from corporate debts and legal judgments. Creditors and garnishers can go after the assets of the LLC itself, but generally cannot go after members' personal assets, such as homes, cars, or personal savings.

Example: If GreenThumb Gardens LLC is sued for accidentally damaging a client's property, the lawsuit is against the LLC, not the members personally. The members' personal assets are usually not at risk to satisfy any legal judgments against the LLC.

Maintaining the Corporate Veil:

The protection offered by limited liability is sometimes referred to as the "corporate veil." To maintain this protection, it's crucial to adhere to certain formalities and practices:

Separate Finances: Keep business and personal finances separate. This means having a dedicated business bank account and not using business funds for personal expenses.

Proper Documentation: Document all business decisions and maintain accurate records. This includes having a written Operating Agreement, keeping minutes of meetings, and recording any major business decisions.

Compliance: Ensure compliance with all legal and regulatory requirements, such as obtaining necessary licenses and permits, filing annual reports, and paying taxes.

Piercing the Corporate Veil:

There are circumstances where courts may "pierce the corporate veil," holding members personally liable. This can happen if members commingle personal and business funds, fail to follow proper business formalities, or engage in fraudulent or illegal activities.

Example: If a member of GreenThumb Gardens LLC uses the LLC's bank account to pay for personal expenses and fails to maintain proper business records, a court might pierce the corporate veil, exposing the member's personal assets to liability.

Limitations of Liability Protection:

While limited liability offers significant protection, it's not absolute. Members may still be personally liable in certain situations:

Personal Guarantees: If a member personally guarantees a loan or contract, they are personally responsible for that obligation.

Personal Actions: If a member personally injures someone or acts in a wrongful or illegal manner, they can be held personally liable.

Professional Malpractice: In some professions, members can be personally liable for malpractice or professional misconduct.

Conclusion:

Limited liability is a cornerstone of the LLC structure, offering members protection for their personal assets against business-related debts and legal judgments. However, maintaining this protection requires careful adherence to business formalities and practices. Understanding the limitations and responsibilities associated with limited liability is crucial for any LLC member.

Sec. 1.3: Flexibility in Management

Unlike corporations, which have a fixed management structure, LLCs offer flexibility. You can run your LLC all by yourself (a single-member LLC) or with a group of people (a multi-member LLC). Plus, you get to decide whether members manage the LLC or if you appoint managers to handle the day-to-day operations.

Unlike corporations, which are required to have a board of directors and corporate officers, LLCs can be managed in various ways to suit the needs of its members. This section will explore the different management structures available to LLCs and the advantages of each.

Member-Managed LLCs:

In a member-managed LLC, all members (owners) participate in the day-to-day management of the business. This is similar to a partnership, where each member has the authority to make decisions on behalf of the LLC.

Example: GreenThumb Gardens LLC might be member-managed, with all three members sharing responsibility for making business decisions, managing finances, and dealing with clients.

Advantages: This structure is straightforward and allows for direct control by the members. It's often preferred in smaller LLCs where all members are actively involved in the business.

Manager-Managed LLCs:

In a manager-managed LLC, members appoint one or more

managers to handle the business's daily operations. Managers can be members or outside parties.

Example: If GreenThumb Gardens LLC grows and the members want to focus on strategic decisions, they might hire a professional manager to oversee daily operations.

Advantages: This structure allows members to be more passive investors and can be beneficial if the members don't have the time or expertise to manage the business. It's also useful if the LLC has a large number of members.

Flexibility in Decision-Making:

LLCs can customize their decision-making processes. The Operating Agreement can specify how decisions are made, whether by majority vote, unanimous consent, or some other method.

Example: GreenThumb Gardens LLC's Operating Agreement might require a unanimous vote for major decisions, like taking out a loan, but allow individual members to make smaller decisions independently.

Advantages: This flexibility allows LLCs to tailor their decision-making processes to their specific needs and preferences.

Distribution of Profits and Losses:

LLCs have flexibility in how they distribute profits and losses among members. Unlike corporations, where dividends are distributed based on share ownership, LLCs can allocate profits and losses in any manner agreed upon by the members.

Example: Even if all three members of GreenThumb Gardens LLC have equal ownership, they might agree to allocate profits differently based on each member's contribution to the business.

Advantages: This flexibility allows for customized profit-sharing arrangements that can incentivize members based on their contributions or investment in the business.

Conclusion:

The flexibility in management is a significant advantage of the LLC structure. It allows members to structure their business in a way that best suits their needs, whether they prefer a hands-on approach or wish to delegate management responsibilities. This flexibility extends to decision-making processes and the distribution of profits and losses, making the LLC an adaptable and attractive option for many business owners.

Sec. 1.4: Tax Advantages

LLCs are known for their tax flexibility. By default, they're treated as "pass-through" entities for tax purposes, meaning the business itself doesn't pay taxes. Instead, the profits and losses "pass through" to the owners' personal tax returns. This setup helps avoid the double taxation often seen in corporations. And if it suits your financial situation better, you can even choose for your LLC to be taxed like a corporation. This section will explore the various tax benefits associated with the LLC structure.

Pass-Through Taxation:

One of the primary tax advantages of an LLC is pass-through taxation. This means that the LLC itself is not taxed at the corporate level. Instead, profits and losses are "passed through" to the members and reported on their personal tax returns.

Example: If GreenThumb Gardens LLC earns a profit, that profit is divided among the members according to their ownership stakes or as stipulated in the Operating Agreement. Each member then reports their share of the profit on their personal tax return.

Advantages: Pass-through taxation avoids the double taxation faced by C corporations, where the corporation is taxed on its profits, and shareholders are taxed again on dividends.

Self-Employment Tax Savings:

In certain cases, LLC members can save on self-employment taxes. While all business income is subject to self-employment taxes, an LLC can elect to be taxed as an S corporation, allowing members to be treated as employees for tax purposes.

Example: Members of GreenThumb Gardens LLC might decide to pay themselves a reasonable salary and take additional profits as distributions, which are not subject to self-employment taxes.

Advantages: This can result in significant tax savings, particularly for LLCs with high profits.

Flexibility in Tax Classification:

LLCs have the flexibility to choose how they are taxed. By default, they are treated as pass-through entities, but they can elect to be taxed as a C corporation or S corporation if it's more advantageous.

Example: If GreenThumb Gardens LLC finds that corporate taxation would be more beneficial due to lower corporate tax rates or the desire to retain earnings in the business, it can elect to be taxed as a C corporation.

Advantages: This flexibility allows LLCs to choose the tax classification that minimizes their tax liability based on their specific circumstances.

Deductible Business Expenses:

LLC members can deduct legitimate business expenses, reducing their taxable income. This includes costs like rent, utilities, supplies, and equipment necessary for running the business.

Example: GreenThumb Gardens LLC can deduct the cost of gardening tools, employee salaries, and advertising expenses, lowering its taxable income.

Advantages: Deducting business expenses can significantly reduce the tax burden for LLC members.

Conclusion:

The tax advantages of an LLC can be substantial, offering flexibility and potential savings. Pass-through taxation, self-employment tax savings, flexibility in tax classification, and the ability to deduct business expenses all contribute to the tax efficiency of the LLC structure. However, tax laws are complex, and the best approach depends on the specific circumstances of each business. It's advisable for LLC members to consult with a tax professional to optimize their tax strategy.

Sec. 1.5: Simplicity and Ease

Starting and maintaining an LLC is generally simpler and requires less paperwork than a corporation. This makes it an attractive option for small business owners who want protection and flexibility without too much complexity. This section will explore the straightforward nature of LLCs and the benefits it offers to business owners.

Ease of Formation:

Setting up an LLC is generally simpler and more straightforward than forming a corporation. The process involves fewer steps and less complex paperwork.

Example: To form GreenThumb Gardens LLC, the members need to file Articles of Organization with the state and pay a filing fee. This is typically less cumbersome than the extensive documentation required for incorporating a business.

Advantages: The ease of formation makes LLCs accessible to a wider range of business owners, including those who may not have extensive legal or business knowledge.

Flexibility in Operating Agreement:

LLCs are not bound by rigid corporate bylaws. Instead, they operate under an Operating Agreement, which members can tailor to fit their specific needs and preferences.

Example: GreenThumb Gardens LLC's Operating Agreement can specify unique profit-sharing arrangements, management structures, and member responsibilities that suit the specific dynamics of the business.

Advantages: This flexibility allows LLC members to create a governance structure that aligns with their business goals and operational style.

Fewer Ongoing Formalities:

LLCs are not subject to the same level of ongoing formalities as corporations. They are not required to hold annual meetings, keep minutes, or have a board of directors.

Example: While GreenThumb Gardens LLC should keep accurate records and adhere to its Operating Agreement, it is not obligated to hold formal annual meetings or record minutes unless it chooses to do so.

Advantages: The reduced formalities save time and resources, allowing members to focus on running the business rather than on administrative tasks.

Easier Management:

LLCs offer a more straightforward management structure, especially for small businesses. Members can manage the business themselves or appoint managers without the need for a formal board of directors.

Example: The members of GreenThumb Gardens LLC can directly oversee daily operations or appoint a manager to handle certain aspects of the business, without the need for a complex management hierarchy.

Advantages: This ease of management is particularly beneficial for small businesses and startups that require agility and quick decision-making.

Conclusion:

The simplicity and ease of an LLC make it an attractive option for many business owners. From formation to daily operations, LLCs offer a streamlined and flexible approach that can save time, reduce complexity, and allow members to focus on what matters most—growing their business.

Sec. 1.6: Professional Appearance

Forming an LLC not only provides legal and financial benefits, but also enhances a company's professional image. The presence of "LLC" at the end of your company name can add a level of professionalism and credibility. It signals to customers, vendors and investors the seriousness of your business. This section will discuss how forming an LLC can contribute to a business's credibility and professional appearance.

Enhanced Credibility:

Having "LLC" in a business name can signal to customers, suppliers, and investors that the business is a legitimate and serious enterprise.

Example: "GreenThumb Gardens LLC" immediately conveys a sense of professionalism and permanence, suggesting that the business is well-established and trustworthy.

Advantages: Enhanced credibility can lead to increased trust from customers and potentially more business opportunities.

Attracting Investors:

Investors often prefer to put their money into a business that has a formal legal structure. An LLC can make a business more attractive to potential investors or partners.

Example: If GreenThumb Gardens LLC seeks outside investment, the LLC structure assures investors that there is a clear legal framework governing their investment.

Advantages: Attracting investment can be crucial for growth and expansion, and the professional appearance of an LLC can facilitate this process.

Separation of Personal and Business Identity:

Forming an LLC creates a clear distinction between the owners and the business, which can enhance the business's professional image.

Example: By operating as GreenThumb Gardens LLC, the members demonstrate that the business is a separate entity, not just an extension of their personal hobbies or interests.

Advantages: This separation can help in establishing a strong brand identity and professional reputation.

Greater Confidence in Business Relationships:

Suppliers, vendors, and other business partners may feel more confident entering into contracts with an LLC compared to a sole proprietorship or partnership.

Example: Suppliers may be more willing to offer favorable terms or credit to GreenThumb Gardens LLC, knowing that it is a legally recognized business entity.

Advantages: Strong business relationships are essential for successful operations, and the professional appearance of an LLC can help build and maintain these relationships.

Conclusion:

The professional appearance of an LLC can have significant benefits for a business. It enhances credibility, attracts investors, separates personal and business identities, and fosters confidence in business relationships. These factors can contribute to the overall success and growth of the business.

Sec. 1.7: State-Specific Rules

While LLCs share many common characteristics, it's important to recognize that each state in the U.S. has its own set of rules and regulations governing LLCs. This section will explore the implications of state-specific rules for LLCs and why understanding these differences is crucial. It's important to familiarize yourself with the specific requirements and benefits offered in the state where you plan to form your LLC.

Variation in Formation Requirements:

The process and requirements for forming an LLC can vary significantly from state to state.

Example: Some states may require additional paperwork or specific information in the Articles of Organization that others do not. For instance, New York requires LLCs to publish a notice of formation in a local newspaper, while most other states do not have this requirement.

Advantages: Understanding the specific requirements in your state ensures that your LLC is properly formed and compliant from the start.

Differences in Fees and Taxes:

States can differ in the fees they charge for forming and maintaining an LLC, as well as in their tax structures.

Example: The initial filing fee and annual report fees can vary widely. Additionally, some states, like California, impose an annual franchise tax on LLCs, while others do not.

Advantages: Being aware of the financial obligations in your state helps in budgeting and financial planning for your LLC.

Distinct Operating Agreement Provisions:

State laws may dictate certain default rules for LLCs, but these can often be overridden by provisions in the Operating Agreement.

Example: Some states have default rules regarding profit distribution or member management, but members of GreenThumb Gardens LLC can specify their own rules in the Operating Agreement, provided they don't violate state law.

Advantages: Customizing the Operating Agreement to suit your specific needs can provide greater control over your LLC, but it's important to ensure it aligns with state laws.

Nuances in Liability and Legal Protections:

The extent of liability protection and the legal precedents for LLCs can differ by state.

Example: Some states may offer stronger protections against creditors or have more favorable legal interpretations for LLC members.

Advantages: Understanding the legal landscape in your state can help in structuring your LLC for maximum protection.

Conclusion:

State-specific rules can have a significant impact on the formation, operation, and legal protections of an LLC. It's essential for prospective and current LLC members to familiarize themselves with the laws and regulations in their state to ensure compliance and to take full advantage of the benefits offered by the LLC structure.

Sec. 1.8: In which state should I form my own LLC?

Dear Reader, I am sure you have two questions running through your mind right now: "Can a U.S. citizen form an LLC in the U.S. state of his choice?"

The answer is, "Yes, he can."

"And in which state is it convenient for me to form my LLC?"

We will also fully answer this legitimate question, but since there are some variables to consider, we will do so in its own section in a few pages.

What you need to know, however, is that **it is true that a U.S. citizen can form an LLC in any state in the United States, regardless of the state in which he or she resides**. In fact, many entrepreneurs choose to form their LLCs in states that offer specific advantages, such as lower taxes, less red tape, or greater protections for LLC members.

It is important to note, however, that if an LLC formed in one state does business in another state, it may need to register in that state as a **"foreign LLC"**. This may result in additional taxes and compliance requirements. In addition, the LLC will be subject to the laws of the state in which it operates, not just the laws of the state in which it was formed.

For example, Delaware is known for its business-friendly legal system, its clear and flexible LLC laws, and its specialized business court, the Court of Chancery. While the states of Wyoming and Nevada, for example, are two popular states for LLC formation, in part because of their favorable tax policies and the privacy offered to LLC members.

Therefore, while it is possible to form an LLC in any state, it is advisable to carefully **consider where you plan to conduct most of your business activities** and which states offer the best advantages for your specific business needs.

Conclusion of Chapter 1:

Now that you understand the basics of what an LLC is and the benefits it offers, you're better equipped to decide if it's the right structure for your business. Remember, the choice you make will lay the groundwork for your business's legal and financial future, so consider it carefully. Ready to learn more? Let's move on to how you can set up your very own LLC!

2. Chapter 2: Setting Up Your LLC

Congratulations on deciding to start your own LLC! This chapter will guide you through the essential steps to bring your LLC from just an idea to a legally recognized business. Let's get your business off the ground!

Sec. 2.1: Choosing the Right Name

Your LLC's name is its first impression, so make it count! It should be unique, memorable, and comply with your state's naming requirements. It's not just a label; it's the first impression your business makes on potential customers and partners. Typically, you'll need to include "LLC" or "Limited Liability Company" in the name to clearly indicate your business structure. Before settling on a name, check your state's business database to make sure it's not already taken. This section will guide you through the process of choosing an appropriate name and provide online resources for checking availability.

Reflecting Your Business:

Your LLC's name should reflect the nature of your business and be easily identifiable to your target audience.

Example: If GreenThumb Gardens LLC specializes in organic gardening, the name should convey this focus to attract customers interested in organic products.

Advantages: A name that aligns with your business's identity can enhance brand recognition and marketing efforts.

Compliance with State Regulations:

Each state has specific naming requirements for LLCs. Generally, the name must include "LLC" or a similar indicator and cannot be misleading or identical to an existing business.

Example: If there's already a "GreenThumb Gardens LLC" in your state, you'll need to choose a different name.

Advantages: Ensuring compliance with state regulations avoids legal issues and the need for a costly rebranding later on.

Uniqueness and Availability:

Before settling on a name, you need to ensure it's unique and not already in use by another business. Most states provide online databases where you can search for business names.

Online Resources:

- **U.S. Patent and Trademark Office (USPTO)**: https://www.uspto.gov/ Check if the name is trademarked at a federal level.

- **Secretary of State's** website: https://www.usa.gov/state-governor Most states have an online business entity search tool where you can check the availability of your desired name.

- **NAICS Association's Free Business Lookup Tool**: https://www.naics.com/search/ Provides a free search tool to check for business names across multiple states.

Domain Availability:

In today's digital age, having an online presence is crucial. Check if the domain name corresponding to your LLC name is available. Online Resources:

Namecheap: https://www.namecheap.com/

Google Domains: https://domains.squarespace.com/

Social Media Handles: Check if the social media handles related to your LLC name are available on platforms where you plan to market your business.

Online Resources: Namechk: https://namechk.com/

Conclusion:

Choosing the right name for your LLC involves ensuring it reflects your business, complies with state regulations, is unique, and has available domains and social media handles. Utilizing online resources to check the availability of your chosen name is an essential step in the formation process.

Sec. 2.2: Appointing a Registered Agent

A registered agent is your LLC's official contact person and is responsible for receiving legal documents on behalf of your company. You can act as your own registered agent, appoint someone you trust, or hire a professional service. The key is that the registered agent must be available during regular business hours and have a physical address in the state where your LLC is formed. A registered agent is a crucial component of maintaining an LLC's legal compliance. This section will explain the role of a registered agent, why it's necessary, and how to appoint one.

Role of a Registered Agent:

A registered agent is an individual or business entity designated to receive legal documents, government correspondence, and compliance-related notices on behalf of your LLC.

Example: If GreenThumb Gardens LLC is sued or subpoenaed, the registered agent will receive the legal documents and notify the LLC members.

Advantages: Having a registered agent ensures that important legal and tax documents are received and handled promptly, reducing the risk of missed deadlines or legal complications.

Requirements for a Registered Agent:

The registered agent must have a physical address (not a P.O. Box) in the state where the LLC is formed and be available during normal business hours.

Example: If GreenThumb Gardens LLC is formed in California, the registered agent must have a physical address in California and be available from 9 am to 5 pm, Monday through Friday.

Advantages: This ensures that the LLC can always be reached through its registered agent, maintaining good standing with the state.

Who Can Serve as a Registered Agent:

An LLC member, a friend, a family member, or a professional registered agent service can serve as a registered agent, provided they meet the state's requirements.

Example: A member of GreenThumb Gardens LLC could serve as the registered agent, or the LLC could hire a professional service that specializes in this role.

Advantages: Professional registered agent services offer privacy, reliability, and expertise in handling legal documents, which can be especially beneficial for LLCs without a fixed office location or those operating in multiple states.

Changing a Registered Agent:

If necessary, an LLC can change its registered agent by filing the appropriate form with the state and paying a small fee.

Example: If the original registered agent for GreenThumb Gardens LLC moves out of state or is no longer able to fulfill their duties, the LLC can appoint a new agent by notifying the state.

Advantages: The ability to change registered agents provides flexibility and ensures that the LLC can maintain compliance even if circumstances change.

To find a registered agent for your LLC, you can use several online resources. Many professional services offer registered agent representation in every state in the United States. Here are some reliable resources where you can search and compare registered agent services. Please note that the author of this guide has no affiliation with the following services; they are listed to assist you in your research.

- LegalZoom: www.legalzoom.com is one of the most popular online legal services providers and offers registered agent services in every state.

- Northwest Registered Agent: www.northwestregisteredagent.com specializes in registered agent services and offers a wide range of support services for LLCs.

- Incfile: www.incfile.com offers LLC and registered agent training services, often with special offers for new clients.

- Rocket Lawyer: www.rocketlawyer.com offers a variety of legal services, including registered agent, with the option of legal counsel.

- Harbor Compliance: www.harborcompliance.com provides registered agent and compliance services for LLCs, with an emphasis on customization of services.

- BizFilings: www.bizfilings.com is another provider of

corporate training and registered agent services, with useful tools to help you manage your LLC.

When choosing a registered agent, consider factors such as cost, reputation, experience, and additional services offered. Many of these providers offer packages that include formation of your LLC and representation as a registered agent, which can simplify the process of starting your business.

Keep in mind that although there are costs associated with using a professional registered agent service, it can provide benefits such as increased privacy, convenience, and the peace of mind of knowing that all legal and governmental communications are being handled professionally.

Conclusion:

Appointing a reliable registered agent is a critical step in forming and maintaining an LLC. The registered agent serves as the LLC's official point of contact for legal and state correspondence, ensuring that the business stays informed and compliant with state regulations.

Sec. 2.3: Filing the Articles of Organization

The Articles of Organization, also known as the Certificate of Formation in some states, is the foundational document that officially forms your LLC.

Think of the Articles of Organization as your LLC's birth certificate. This document officially registers your LLC with the state. While the specifics can vary, it generally includes your LLC's name, address, registered agent information, and sometimes the names of the members. You'll file this document with your state's business filing office and pay a filing fee, which can range from relatively modest to a few hundred dollars.

This section will guide you through the process of preparing and filing this crucial document.

Understanding the Articles of Organization:

The Articles of Organization is a legal document that outlines the basic information about your LLC and is filed with the state government.

Example: For GreenThumb Gardens LLC, the Articles of Organization will include the LLC's name, address, registered agent information, and the names of its members.

Advantages: Filing this document is what legally establishes your LLC, providing you with the benefits of limited liability and a formal business structure.

Preparing the Document:

Most states provide a standard form for the Articles of Organization, which can be downloaded from the state's Secretary of State website or business division.

Example: GreenThumb Gardens LLC can download the form from the California Secretary of State's website, fill it out, and ensure all required information is included.

Advantages: Using the state-provided form simplifies the process and helps ensure that all necessary information is included.

Filing Fees and Procedures:

Each state has its own filing fees and procedures for submitting the Articles of Organization. Some states allow online filing, while others may require a mailed or hand-delivered hard copy.

Example: GreenThumb Gardens LLC will need to pay a filing fee (which varies by state) and may have the option to file online for faster processing.

Advantages: Understanding the specific filing procedures and fees in your state helps you budget appropriately and avoid delays.

Online Resources for Filing:

Many states offer online portals where you can file the Articles of Organization electronically.

In the previous section we provided a list of online resources useful for this purpose.

As for the timing, it varies from 24/48 hours to a few days at the most, depending on the state in which you are registering your LLC.

After Filing:

Once the Articles of Organization are filed and approved, your LLC is officially formed. You will receive a confirmation, usually in the form of a stamped copy of the Articles or a certificate of formation.

Example: After filing, GreenThumb Gardens LLC will receive a certificate from the state confirming its official status as an LLC.

Advantages: This confirmation serves as legal proof of your LLC's existence and is often required for opening business bank accounts, applying for loans, and other business activities.

Conclusion:

Filing the Articles of Organization is a critical step in forming your LLC. It involves preparing the document with accurate information, understanding state-specific filing procedures and fees, and utilizing available online resources to streamline the process. Once filed and approved, your business is officially recognized as an LLC, providing you with the legal framework to operate and grow your business.

Sec. 2.4: Crafting Your Operating Agreement

An Operating Agreement is a critical document for any LLC, detailing the ownership structure, operational procedures, and guidelines for resolving disputes. While not always legally required, it's highly recommended for ensuring smooth operations and protecting the interests of all members.

It's like a rulebook that outlines how your LLC will be run. It covers the ownership structure, member roles, profit distribution, and what happens if a member wants to leave the LLC. Having this agreement in place can prevent misunderstandings and disputes down the line.

Purpose of an Operating Agreement:

The Operating Agreement serves as a contract among the members of the LLC, outlining how the business will be run and what happens in various scenarios.

Example: GreenThumb Gardens LLC's Operating Agreement might specify how profits are distributed, what happens if a member wants to leave the business, and how decisions are made.

Advantages: A well-crafted Operating Agreement can prevent misunderstandings and disputes among members by clearly defining rights, responsibilities, and procedures.

Key Components of an Operating Agreement:

While Operating Agreements can vary widely, certain key components are generally included:

Ownership Structure: Details the percentage of ownership each member has in the LLC.

Profit Distribution: Outlines how profits and losses will be distributed among members.

Management Structure: Specifies whether the LLC will be member-managed or manager-managed.

Voting Rights and Procedures: Establishes how decisions are made and the voting power of each member.

Provisions for Adding or Removing Members: Sets the rules for how new members can join and existing members can exit the LLC.

Dissolution Procedures: Outlines the process for dissolving the LLC if necessary.

Tailoring to Your Business Needs:

The Operating Agreement should be tailored to the specific needs and preferences of your LLC.

Example: GreenThumb Gardens LLC might decide that all major decisions require a unanimous vote, while another LLC might only require a majority.

Advantages: Customizing the Operating Agreement ensures that it aligns with the unique goals and operations of your business.

State-Specific Considerations:

Some states have default rules that apply to LLCs unless explicitly overridden in the Operating Agreement.

Example: If GreenThumb Gardens LLC doesn't specify a different profit distribution method, the state may default to an equal distribution among members.

Advantages: Being aware of state-specific rules ensures that your Operating Agreement covers all necessary areas and avoids unintended default rules.

Legal Assistance:

While it's possible to draft an Operating Agreement on your own, seeking legal assistance can ensure that the document is comprehensive and legally sound.

Online Resources, search for these services on search engines: LegalZoom, Rocket Lawyer, Nolo

Local attorneys specializing in business law.

Conclusion:

Crafting an Operating Agreement is a vital step in establishing your LLC. It provides a clear framework for the operation of the business, outlines the rights and responsibilities of members, and helps prevent disputes. Tailoring the agreement to your business needs and considering state-specific rules are key to creating an effective document.

Sec. 2.5: Obtaining Licenses and Permits

After forming your LLC, the next step is to ensure you have all the necessary licenses and permits to legally operate your business. This section will guide you through identifying and obtaining the required documentation. Depending on your business type and location, you might need certain licenses and permits. This could include a general business license, professional licenses, or even health and safety permits. Check with your local and state government to find out what's required for your specific business.

Understanding Business Licenses and Permits:

Licenses and permits are official approvals from various government agencies that allow your LLC to carry out certain activities.

Example: GreenThumb Gardens LLC may need a general business license to operate, a seller's permit to sell products, and possibly a special environmental permit if they're using certain chemicals.

Advantages: Obtaining the necessary licenses and permits ensures that your business is compliant with local, state, and federal regulations, avoiding fines and legal issues.

Types of Licenses and Permits:

The types of licenses and permits required can vary greatly depending on the nature of your business, your location, and the regulations of various government agencies.

General Business License: Required by most cities or counties to legally operate a business within their jurisdiction.

Professional and Occupational Licenses: Specific to certain professions and occupations that require additional training or certification.

Health and Safety Permits: Often required for businesses that prepare or sell food, or those that may impact public health.

Environmental Permits: Necessary for businesses that may have an environmental impact, such as those dealing with hazardous materials.

Signage Permits: Required for businesses that want to put up signs larger than a certain size.

Building and Zoning Permits: Needed if you plan to construct a new building or alter an existing one for your business.

Researching Your Requirements:

To determine the specific licenses and permits your LLC needs, you'll need to conduct thorough research.

Online Resources:

- U.S. Small Business Administration (SBA) License/Permit:https://www.sba.gov/business-guide/launch-your-business/apply-licenses-permits
- Your state's Secretary of State website or business division.
- Your local city or county government website.

Advantages: Proper research ensures that you're fully aware of all the licenses and permits required for your business, helping you avoid legal complications.

Application Process:

Once you've identified the necessary licenses and permits, you'll need to complete the application process for each one, which may involve filling out forms, paying fees, and possibly undergoing inspections.

Example: GreenThumb Gardens LLC will need to fill out an application for a general business license with their city, pay the required fee, and wait for approval before they can begin operations.

Advantages: Understanding the application process and timelines helps you plan accordingly and ensures that your business can start operations without unnecessary delays.

Maintaining Compliance:

Many licenses and permits need to be renewed periodically, and it's important to stay informed about any changes in regulations that may affect your business.

Example: GreenThumb Gardens LLC should set reminders for when their licenses and permits are up for renewal and stay updated on any new regulations that may affect their business.

Advantages: Staying on top of renewals and regulatory changes helps maintain your business's legal compliance and uninterrupted operations.

Conclusion:

Obtaining the necessary licenses and permits is a critical step in establishing your LLC. It involves researching your specific requirements, completing the application process, and maintaining compliance through renewals and staying informed about regulatory changes. Ensuring that your business has all the required documentation in place is essential for legal operation and long-term success.

Sec. 2.6: EIN and Tax Registration

Once your LLC is legally formed, the next crucial step is to register for taxes and obtain an Employer Identification Number (EIN), which is like a Social Security number for your business. You'll use this number to open a business bank account, hire employees, and file taxes. Applying for an EIN is free and can be done online through the IRS website.

This section will guide you through the process of tax registration and the importance of an EIN for your LLC.

Understanding the EIN:

An Employer Identification Number (EIN), also known as a Federal Tax Identification Number, is a unique nine-digit number assigned by the Internal Revenue Service (IRS) to businesses for tax purposes.

Example: GreenThumb Gardens LLC will use its EIN for all federal tax filings, opening a business bank account, and hiring employees.

Advantages: An EIN is essential for maintaining your LLC's corporate veil, separating your personal and business finances, and complying with IRS requirements.

Obtaining an EIN:

The process of obtaining an EIN is straightforward and can be done online, by mail, or by fax.

Online Resources:

IRS EIN Online Application:

https://www.irs.gov/businesses/small-businesses-self-employed/apply-for-an-employer-identification-number-ein-online

Example: GreenThumb Gardens LLC can apply for an EIN through the IRS website, and typically receive their EIN immediately after completing the application.

Advantages: Applying online is the fastest way to obtain an EIN, and it's free of charge.

State Tax Registration:

In addition to federal taxes, your LLC may need to register for state taxes, such as sales tax, payroll tax, or others, depending on the nature of your business and your state's regulations.

Online Resources:

Your state's Department of Revenue or equivalent agency.

Example: If GreenThumb Gardens LLC sells products, it will need to register for sales tax in the state where it operates.

Advantages: Registering for state taxes ensures compliance with state laws and avoids penalties or fines.

International Considerations:

If your LLC will be doing business internationally, you may need to consider additional tax registrations or treaties that could affect your tax obligations.

Example: GreenThumb Gardens LLC may need to understand import/export taxes if they plan to buy or sell goods internationally.

Advantages: Being aware of international tax obligations helps avoid legal complications and ensures proper tax handling.

Maintaining Good Standing:

Regularly filing tax returns and paying any owed taxes is crucial for keeping your LLC in good standing with both federal and state tax authorities.

Example: GreenThumb Gardens LLC should keep accurate financial records and file all necessary tax returns on time, whether monthly, quarterly, or annually, depending on the tax type.

Advantages: Staying in good standing with tax authorities avoids penalties and ensures your LLC can continue operating smoothly.

Conclusion:

Obtaining an EIN and registering for taxes are essential steps in establishing your LLC. An EIN is necessary for federal tax purposes, hiring employees, and separating your personal and business finances. Additionally, registering for state taxes ensures compliance with state regulations. Maintaining good standing with tax authorities through timely filings and payments is crucial for the ongoing success of your LLC.

Sec. 2.7: Opening a Business Bank Account

Opening a business bank account is a fundamental step in establishing the financial foundation of your LLC. It separates your personal finances from your business transactions, providing clarity and protection. To keep your personal and business finances separate (which is critical to maintaining your liability protection), open a bank account solely for your LLC. You'll typically need your EIN, articles of organization, and operating agreement.

This section will walk you through the process of setting up a business bank account for your LLC.

Importance of a Business Bank Account:

A business bank account helps to maintain the corporate veil, ensuring that your personal assets are protected from business liabilities.

Example: GreenThumb Gardens LLC will use its business bank account for all business-related transactions, keeping them separate from the personal finances of its members.

Advantages: This separation simplifies accounting, enhances professionalism, and is crucial for tax purposes.

Requirements for Opening an Account:

To open a business bank account, you'll need several documents and pieces of information.

Employer Identification Number (EIN): Your LLC's EIN is required for tax identification purposes.

Articles of Organization: The document that officially formed your LLC.

Operating Agreement: Some banks may require a copy of your LLC's Operating Agreement.

Business License: Proof of your business's legal right to operate.

Identification: Personal identification documents of the account signatories.

Choosing the Right Bank:

Consider the following factors when choosing a bank for your business account:

Fees: Seek out accounts that offer low or no monthly charges.

Minimum Balance Requirements: Be aware that some accounts necessitate maintaining a minimum balance to bypass additional fees.

Online Banking Features: Ensure the bank offers robust online banking tools.

Additional Services: Consider if you need merchant services, credit lines, or other banking products.

Setting Up the Account:

Once you've gathered all necessary documents and chosen a bank, you can set up your account. This can often be done online, but some banks may require you to visit a branch in person.

Example: GreenThumb Gardens LLC can apply for a business bank account online with their chosen bank, uploading the necessary documents through the bank's secure portal.

Advantages: A business bank account allows you to manage your finances efficiently, accept payments, and pay bills related to your LLC.

Maintaining the Account:

Regularly review your account statements, reconcile transactions, and keep your banking information secure.

Example: GreenThumb Gardens LLC should designate a member to oversee the account, ensuring that all transactions are recorded and reconciled with the LLC's financial records.

Advantages: Diligent account maintenance helps prevent fraud, ensures accurate bookkeeping, and contributes to the financial health of your LLC.

Conclusion:

Opening and maintaining a business bank account is essential for the financial management of your LLC. It provides a clear separation between personal and business finances, aids in bookkeeping, and is necessary for tax purposes. By choosing the right bank and managing the account responsibly, you set a solid financial foundation for your LLC.

Conclusion of Chapter 2:

By following these steps, you'll have laid a strong foundation for your LLC. Each step is crucial in ensuring that your business is set up correctly and legally. With these formalities out of the way, you're ready to focus on running and growing your business. In the next chapter, we'll explore the ins and outs of managing your LLC effectively.

3. Chapter 3: Running Your LLC

Now that your LLC is officially formed, it's time to focus on the day-to-day operations and long-term management of your business. This chapter will cover the essentials of running your LLC smoothly and effectively.

Sec. 3.1: Understanding Your Role

As a member or manager of an LLC, it's crucial to have a clear understanding of your role and responsibilities. As an LLC owner, also known as a member, your role can vary depending on your business's size and structure. In a single-member LLC, you'll handle all aspects of the business. In a multi-member LLC, you may share responsibilities with other members or appoint managers. Clarify each member's role early on to avoid confusion and ensure a smooth operation.

This section will delve into the different roles within an LLC and what they entail.

Member-Managed vs. Manager-Managed LLCs:

LLCs can be structured in two main ways: member-managed or manager-managed.

Member-Managed: In a member-managed LLC, all members (owners) participate in the day-to-day operations and decision-making processes of the business.

Example: In GreenThumb Gardens LLC, if it's member-managed, all members would have a say in daily business decisions, from vendor selection to marketing strategies.

Advantages: This structure allows for direct control by the members and can be beneficial in smaller LLCs where members are actively involved in the business.

Manager-Managed: In a manager-managed LLC, members appoint one or more managers to handle the daily operations, while members take a more passive role.

Example: GreenThumb Gardens LLC might appoint a manager with horticultural expertise to oversee daily operations, while members focus on broader strategic decisions.

Advantages: This structure is useful when members want to invest in the business without being involved in daily management or when specialized management is needed.

Defining Your Role:

Your role in the LLC will depend on its structure and the agreements made between members.

Duties and Responsibilities: Clearly define the duties and responsibilities of each member or manager to avoid confusion and overlap.

Decision-Making: Establish how decisions will be made, whether by majority vote, unanimous consent, or delegated to a manager.

Conflict Resolution: Implement a process for resolving disputes or disagreements within the LLC.

Legal Obligations:

Members and managers have certain legal obligations, including fiduciary duties to the LLC and its members.

Duty of Care: Act with the care an ordinarily prudent person in a similar position would exercise under similar circumstances.

Duty of Loyalty: Put the interests of the LLC above personal interests and avoid conflicts of interest.

Compliance: Ensure the LLC complies with all applicable laws and regulations.

Developing Leadership Skills:

Whether you're a member or a manager, developing strong leadership skills is beneficial for the success of the LLC.

Communication: Effective communication is key to clear decision-making and conflict resolution.

Financial Acumen: Understanding the financial aspects of the business helps in making informed decisions.

Strategic Thinking: Being able to plan and execute long-term strategies contributes to the growth and stability of the LLC.

Conclusion:

Understanding your role within an LLC is fundamental to its successful operation. Whether you're a member or a manager, clear definitions of responsibilities, legal obligations, and effective leadership skills are essential. By comprehensively understanding your role, you contribute to the smooth functioning and success of the LLC.

Sec. 3.2: Making Decisions

Decision-making is a critical aspect of running an LLC. It involves setting strategies, resolving issues, and steering the company towards its goals. Decision-making in an LLC can be flexible. You can opt for member-managed, where all members participate in decision-making, or manager-managed, where appointed managers handle daily operations. Your Operating Agreement should outline the decision-making process, voting rights, and how major decisions are made.

This section will explore the decision-making process within an LLC and provide guidance on establishing effective practices.

Types of Decisions:

Decisions in an LLC can be categorized into two main types:

Daily Operational Decisions: These are routine decisions made in the course of business operations, such as purchasing supplies or setting work schedules.

Example: GreenThumb Gardens LLC decides which supplier to use for soil and fertilizer.

Major Business Decisions: These decisions have a significant impact on the LLC and often require consent from all or a majority of members. They can include taking out loans, entering into significant contracts, or selling the business.

Example: GreenThumb Gardens LLC considers expanding to a new location, which requires a substantial investment.

Decision-Making Authority:

The authority to make decisions will depend on the LLC's management structure.

Member-Managed: In a member-managed LLC, all members typically have equal decision-making authority, unless the Operating Agreement specifies otherwise.

Manager-Managed: In a manager-managed LLC, the appointed manager(s) have the authority to make operational decisions, while members retain authority over major business decisions.

Decision-Making Processes:

Establishing clear processes for making decisions is crucial for the smooth operation of the LLC.

Voting: Define the voting rights of each member and the required majority for different types of decisions.

Meetings: Hold regular meetings to discuss and make decisions, ensuring all members have the opportunity to participate.

Record-Keeping: Keep detailed records of all decisions made, including meeting minutes and written consents.

Factors to Consider:

When making decisions, consider the following factors:

Legal Implications: Ensure that decisions comply with laws and regulations.

Financial Impact: Assess the financial consequences of decisions on the LLC's bottom line.

Long-Term Goals: Align decisions with the LLC's long-term objectives and strategies.

Risk Assessment: Evaluate the risks associated with decisions and plan for mitigation.

Conflict Resolution:

Disagreements are inevitable in any business. Establishing a conflict resolution process can help resolve disputes effectively.

Mediation: Consider using a neutral third party to mediate disputes.

Operating Agreement: Refer to the Operating Agreement for guidance on resolving conflicts.

Compromise: Encourage a culture of compromise and collaboration among members.

Conclusion:

Effective decision-making is vital for the success of an LLC. It involves understanding the types of decisions, establishing clear processes, considering various factors, and resolving conflicts. By implementing structured decision-making practices, an LLC can navigate challenges and capitalize on opportunities, driving the business towards its goals.

Sec. 3.3: Managing Finances

Effective financial management is the backbone of any successful LLC. It involves budgeting, accounting, and making informed financial decisions. Good financial management is key to your LLC's success. This includes budgeting, bookkeeping, and tax planning. Consider using accounting software to track your finances accurately. Also, remember to keep your personal and business finances separate to maintain your liability protection.

This section will cover the essentials of managing your LLC's finances.

Setting Up an Accounting System:

An organized accounting system is crucial for tracking income, expenses, and overall financial health.

Software Solutions: Consider using accounting software like QuickBooks or FreshBooks to streamline financial tracking.

Bookkeeping Basics: Maintain accurate records of all financial transactions, including sales, purchases, and payments.

Example: GreenThumb Gardens LLC records all transactions related to their landscaping projects, including costs for plants, labor, and equipment.

Budgeting and Forecasting:

Creating a budget helps in planning and controlling financial resources.

Projected Income: Estimate future sales based on market analysis and past performance.

Planned Expenditures: Outline anticipated expenses, such as rent, salaries, and supplies.

Cash Flow Management: Monitor cash flow to ensure the business can cover its short-term obligations.

Example: GreenThumb Gardens LLC prepares a monthly budget to manage seasonal fluctuations in their business.

Financial Reporting:

Regular financial reports provide insights into the LLC's performance and are essential for decision-making.

Income Statement: Shows the LLC's revenues, expenses, and profits over a specific period.

Balance Sheet: Provides a snapshot of the LLC's assets, liabilities, and equity at a given point in time.

Cash Flow Statement: Tracks the flow of cash in and out of the business.

Example: GreenThumb Gardens LLC reviews quarterly financial reports to assess their profitability and adjust their business strategy accordingly.

Tax Planning and Compliance:

Understanding and complying with tax obligations is critical for any LLC.

Tax Filings: Ensure timely and accurate filing of all required tax returns, such as income tax, sales tax, and payroll tax.

Deductions and Credits: Take advantage of any tax deductions and credits for which the LLC is eligible.

Professional Advice: Consider consulting a tax professional for complex tax matters.

Example: GreenThumb Gardens LLC consults a CPA to optimize their tax strategy and ensure compliance with IRS regulations.

Financial Controls:

Implementing financial controls helps prevent fraud and errors.

Segregation of Duties: Divide financial responsibilities among different individuals to reduce the risk of fraud.

Regular Audits: Conduct periodic audits to ensure the accuracy of financial records.

Approval Processes: Establish approval processes for significant expenditures.

Example: GreenThumb Gardens LLC requires two members to sign off on any purchase over $1,000.

Conclusion:

Managing finances effectively is crucial for the sustainability and growth of your LLC. It involves setting up a reliable accounting system, budgeting, preparing financial reports, ensuring tax compliance, and implementing financial controls. By staying on top of your LLC's financial health, you can make informed decisions, plan for the future, and steer your business towards success.

Sec. 3.4: Holding Meetings

Holding regular meetings is a key practice for the effective governance of an LLC. Meetings provide a structured opportunity for members to discuss business matters, make decisions, and plan for the future. Regular meetings can help keep everyone on the same page, especially in a multi-member LLC. Use these meetings to discuss business performance, make decisions, and plan for the future. Documenting these meetings in minutes can provide a clear record of decisions made and actions taken.

This section will guide you through the process of organizing and conducting LLC meetings.

Types of Meetings:

There are generally two types of meetings in an LLC:

Regular Meetings: Scheduled at regular intervals (e.g., monthly, quarterly) to discuss ongoing business operations, review financial reports, and make routine decisions.

Example: GreenThumb Gardens LLC holds monthly meetings to review project progress, financial status, and upcoming business opportunities.

Special Meetings: Called for specific purposes, such as making major business decisions, addressing urgent issues, or amending the Operating Agreement.

Example: GreenThumb Gardens LLC calls a special meeting to discuss a significant investment opportunity.

Preparing for Meetings:

Proper preparation ensures meetings are productive and efficient.

Agenda: Prepare a clear agenda outlining the topics to be discussed and decisions to be made.

Documentation: Provide members with relevant documents, such as financial reports or proposals, in advance.

Scheduling: Choose a time and date that accommodates all members, considering virtual attendance options if necessary.

Conducting Meetings:

Effective meeting management is crucial for productive discussions and decision-making.

Chairperson: Appoint a chairperson to lead the meeting and keep discussions on track.

Minutes: Assign someone to take minutes, recording key discussions, decisions, and action items.

Participation: Encourage active participation from all members, ensuring everyone has the opportunity to voice their opinions.

Voting: Follow the established voting procedures for making decisions, as outlined in the Operating Agreement.

After the Meeting:

The work doesn't end when the meeting concludes.

Distribute Minutes: Share the meeting minutes with all members for review and approval.

Follow-Up: Ensure that action items and decisions are implemented and followed up on.

Record-Keeping: Store minutes and other meeting documents in the LLC's records for future reference.

Virtual Meetings:

In today's digital age, virtual meetings have become increasingly common.

Technology: Utilize video conferencing tools like Zoom or Microsoft Teams to facilitate remote attendance.

Security: Ensure the virtual meeting platform is secure to protect confidential business information.

Accessibility: Make sure all members have access to the necessary technology and are comfortable using it.

Conclusion:

Regular and well-organized meetings are essential for the effective management of an LLC. They provide a platform for members to communicate, make decisions, and align on the business's direction. By preparing thoroughly, conducting meetings efficiently, and following up diligently, you can ensure that your LLC's meetings contribute positively to the business's success.

Sec. 3.5: Complying with Legal Requirements

Adhering to legal requirements is crucial for the legitimacy and smooth operation of your LLC. Compliance ensures that your business is protected from legal disputes and penalties. Stay compliant with state and federal regulations to avoid fines and legal issues. This includes filing annual reports, renewing licenses and permits, and adhering to employment laws if you have employees.

This section will outline the key legal obligations that your LLC must fulfill.

Understanding State Regulations:

Each state has its own set of rules and regulations governing LLCs.

State Filings: Stay up-to-date with annual or biennial reports required by your state to maintain good standing.

State Taxes: Understand and comply with state tax obligations, which may include sales tax, franchise tax, or others.

Example: GreenThumb Gardens LLC files an annual report with the state and pays the necessary state taxes to remain compliant.

Federal Compliance:

Federal regulations also impose certain requirements on LLCs.

Federal Taxes: Ensure compliance with federal tax filings, including income tax returns and employment taxes if you have employees.

Labor Laws: Adhere to federal labor laws if your LLC hires employees, including minimum wage, overtime, and workplace safety regulations.

Example: GreenThumb Gardens LLC files its federal tax returns on time and follows all OSHA guidelines to ensure a safe working environment.

Local Ordinances:

Local governments may have additional regulations that affect your LLC.

Zoning Laws: Ensure your business operations comply with local zoning laws.

Permits and Licenses: Obtain and renew any required local permits or business licenses.

Example: GreenThumb Gardens LLC checks with the local municipality to ensure their landscaping activities are permitted in the areas they serve.

Record-Keeping and Documentation:

Maintaining accurate records is essential for legal compliance.

Operating Agreement: Keep an updated copy of your LLC's Operating Agreement.

Financial Records: Maintain detailed financial records, including income, expenses, and bank statements.

Legal Documents: Store all legal documents, such as contracts, licenses, and permits, in a secure location.

Example: GreenThumb Gardens LLC uses a cloud-based document management system to securely store and access all their business records.

Intellectual Property Protection:

Protecting your LLC's intellectual property (IP) is vital.

Trademarks: Register trademarks for your LLC's name, logo, or product names to protect your brand identity.

Patents: If your LLC creates unique products or processes, consider applying for patents.

Example: GreenThumb Gardens LLC registers its unique logo as a trademark to prevent others from using it without permission.

Data Privacy and Security:

If your LLC collects personal data, ensure compliance with data protection laws.

Privacy Policies: Implement and display a privacy policy if you have a website or collect customer data.

Data Security: Use secure methods to store and handle personal data to prevent breaches.

Example: GreenThumb Gardens LLC has a clear privacy policy on its website and uses encrypted databases to store customer information.

Conclusion:

Complying with legal requirements is a non-negotiable aspect of running an LLC. It involves understanding and adhering to state, federal, and local regulations, maintaining proper records, protecting intellectual property, and ensuring data privacy. By staying informed and proactive about legal compliance, you safeguard your LLC from legal risks and contribute to its long-term success.

Sec. 3.6: Tax Responsibilities

Navigating tax responsibilities is a critical aspect of managing an LLC. Understanding and fulfilling your tax obligations ensures legal compliance and can also provide financial benefits. This may involve paying self-employment taxes, state taxes, and federal income taxes. Consult with a tax professional to ensure you're taking advantage of all available tax benefits and meeting all deadlines. This section will outline the key tax responsibilities for your LLC.

Understanding LLC Taxation:

LLCs offer flexibility in how they are taxed, which can be one of the following:

Disregarded Entity: For single-member LLCs, the IRS treats the LLC as a disregarded entity, meaning the business itself is not taxed. Instead, profits and losses are reported on the owner's personal tax return.

Example: If GreenThumb Gardens LLC is a single-member LLC, the owner would report the business's income and expenses on their personal tax return.

Partnership: Multi-member LLCs are typically taxed as partnerships. The LLC itself does not pay taxes, but profits and losses are passed through to the members, who report them on their personal tax returns.

Example: If GreenThumb Gardens LLC has multiple members, each member would report their share of the profits and losses on their personal tax returns.

Corporation: An LLC can elect to be taxed as a corporation, either as a C corporation or an S corporation, which has different tax implications.

Example: If GreenThumb Gardens LLC elects S corporation status, it can provide payroll to members and potentially save on self-employment taxes.

Federal Tax Responsibilities:

Regardless of the tax classification, there are certain federal tax responsibilities that all LLCs must fulfill.

Income Tax: File the appropriate federal income tax return based on your LLC's tax classification.

Self-Employment Tax: Members of an LLC may be subject to

self-employment tax on their share of the profits.

Employment Taxes: If your LLC has employees, you are responsible for withholding and paying payroll taxes.

Example: GreenThumb Gardens LLC withholds income taxes, Social Security, and Medicare taxes from its employees' paychecks and pays the employer's share of payroll taxes.

State and Local Taxes:

State and local tax obligations can vary significantly depending on your location.

State Income Tax: Some states require LLCs to pay income tax or franchise tax.

Sales Tax: If your LLC sells goods or services, you may need to collect and remit sales tax.

Property Tax: If your LLC owns real property, you may be responsible for property taxes.

Example: GreenThumb Gardens LLC collects sales tax on its landscaping services and remits it to the state.

Quarterly Estimated Taxes:

LLC members may need to make quarterly estimated tax payments to the IRS and state tax authorities.

Calculating Payments: Estimate the amount of tax you will owe for the year and make payments in four installments.

Deadlines: Quarterly estimated tax payments are typically due in April, June, September, and January.

Example: The members of GreenThumb Gardens LLC

calculate their estimated tax liability and make quarterly payments to avoid underpayment penalties.

Tax Deductions and Credits:

Take advantage of tax deductions and credits to reduce your tax liability.

Business Expenses: Deduct legitimate business expenses, such as supplies, equipment, and travel.

Home Office Deduction: If you use part of your home exclusively for business, you may qualify for the home office deduction.

Tax Credits: Explore available tax credits that can directly reduce your tax bill.

Example: GreenThumb Gardens LLC deducts the cost of plants and gardening tools as business expenses on its tax return.

Conclusion:

Managing tax responsibilities is a vital part of running an LLC. It involves understanding how your LLC is taxed, fulfilling federal, state, and local tax obligations, making quarterly estimated tax payments, and taking advantage of deductions and credits. By staying informed and proactive about your tax responsibilities, you can ensure compliance and optimize your LLC's financial health.

Sec. 3.7: Growing Your Business

rowth is a sign of a healthy business. For an LLC, growth can mean expanding services, entering new markets, or increasing profitability. With your LLC up and running, consider strategies for growth. This could involve expanding your product line, entering new markets, or even merging with or acquiring other businesses. Always weigh the potential risks and rewards before making significant growth decisions.

This section will provide strategies and considerations for growing your LLC.

Strategic Planning:

Growth should be intentional and planned.

Business Plan: Update your business plan to include growth strategies and objectives.

Market Research: Conduct research to identify growth opportunities, such as new markets or untapped customer segments.

Example: GreenThumb Gardens LLC identifies a demand for organic gardening services in a nearby city and plans to expand its offerings.

Financial Considerations:

Ensure that your LLC is financially prepared for growth.

Budgeting: Allocate resources for growth initiatives, such as marketing or hiring additional staff.

Funding: Explore funding options, including loans, investors, or reinvesting profits.

Example: GreenThumb Gardens LLC secures a small business loan to finance the purchase of new equipment for its expansion.

Marketing and Sales:

Effective marketing and sales strategies are crucial for growth.

Branding: Strengthen your LLC's brand to stand out in the market.

Marketing Campaigns: Implement targeted marketing campaigns to attract new customers.

Sales Strategies: Develop sales strategies that align with your growth objectives.

Example: GreenThumb Gardens LLC launches a social media campaign to promote its new organic gardening services.

Operational Efficiency:

Streamlining operations can support growth by improving efficiency and reducing costs.

Process Optimization: Review and optimize business processes for efficiency.

Technology: Implement technology solutions to automate tasks and improve productivity.

Example: GreenThumb Gardens LLC adopts a project management software to better coordinate its landscaping projects.

Expanding Products or Services:

Offering new products or services can attract new customers and increase revenue.

Product Development: Develop new products or services that meet customer needs.

Market Testing: Test new offerings in a small segment before a full-scale launch.

Example: GreenThumb Gardens LLC introduces a line of eco-friendly garden supplies and tests them in a pilot market.

Entering New Markets:

Expanding into new geographic or demographic markets can provide new revenue streams.

Market Analysis: Analyze potential new markets for viability and competition.

Localization: Adapt your offerings to meet the specific needs of the new market.

Example: GreenThumb Gardens LLC researches and enters the neighboring state's market, adjusting its services to suit the local climate.

Building Partnerships:

Strategic partnerships can provide growth opportunities.

Collaborations: Partner with other businesses to offer complementary services.

Networking: Build relationships with industry peers, suppliers, and customers.

Example: GreenThumb Gardens LLC partners with a local nursery to offer a wider variety of plants to its customers.

Conclusion:

Growing your LLC requires careful planning, financial readiness, effective marketing, operational efficiency, product expansion, market exploration, and strategic partnerships. By focusing on these areas, you can increase your LLC's market presence, customer base, and profitability, setting the stage for long-term success.

Sec. 3.8: Protecting Your Business

Safeguarding your LLC is crucial for its longevity and success. Protection involves legal, financial, and operational measures to mitigate risks and ensure the business's resilience. Protect your business with the right insurance policies, such as general liability insurance, professional liability insurance, and property insurance. This can safeguard your business against unforeseen events and liabilities.

This section will outline key strategies to protect your LLC.

Legal Protection:

Legal safeguards are essential to protect your business from liabilities and disputes.

Contracts and Agreements: Ensure all business dealings are formalized with clear, legally binding contracts.

Intellectual Property: Protect your LLC's intellectual property, including trademarks, patents, and copyrights.

Compliance: Stay compliant with all relevant laws and regulations to avoid legal penalties.

Example: GreenThumb Gardens LLC registers its unique gardening tool designs as patents to prevent imitation by competitors.

Insurance:

Various types of insurance can shield your LLC from unforeseen events.

General Liability Insurance: Protects against claims of bodily injury or property damage.

Professional Liability Insurance: Covers claims related to errors or negligence in services provided.

Property Insurance: Protects your business property, including equipment and inventory.

Example: GreenThumb Gardens LLC has comprehensive insurance coverage, including general liability and property insurance, to protect against potential accidents or damages.

Financial Safeguards:

Financial health is critical for the protection and stability of your LLC.

Emergency Fund: Maintain a reserve of funds to cover

unexpected expenses or downturns.

Diversification: Diversify income streams to reduce reliance on a single source.

Debt Management: Manage debts wisely to avoid over-leveraging and financial strain.

Example: GreenThumb Gardens LLC sets aside a portion of its profits each month to build an emergency fund.

Data Security:

In the digital age, protecting your business's data is paramount.

Cybersecurity Measures: Implement robust cybersecurity measures to protect against hacking and data breaches.

Data Backup: Regularly backup important business data to prevent loss in case of system failures.

Employee Training: Train employees on best practices for data security and privacy.

Example: GreenThumb Gardens LLC uses encrypted software for customer data and conducts regular cybersecurity training for its staff.

Operational Resilience:

Building a resilient operation helps your LLC withstand challenges.

Business Continuity Planning: Develop a plan to maintain operations during disruptions, such as natural disasters or supply chain issues.

Risk Assessment: Regularly assess potential risks to your business and develop mitigation strategies.

Flexible Operations: Adapt your business model to be flexible in the face of changing market conditions.

Example: GreenThumb Gardens LLC has a business continuity plan that includes backup suppliers and remote work capabilities.

Conclusion:

Protecting your LLC involves a multi-faceted approach, including legal safeguards, insurance, financial stability, data security, and operational resilience. By proactively addressing these areas, you can shield your business from various risks and ensure its long-term viability and success.

Conclusion of Chapter 3:

Running an LLC involves various responsibilities, from managing finances to complying with legal requirements. By staying organized, informed, and proactive, you can navigate the challenges and enjoy the rewards of entrepreneurship. In the next chapter, we'll delve into the specifics of LLC taxation and how to make the most of your business's financial situation.

4. Chapter 4: Taxes and Money

Understanding and managing your LLC's finances and taxes is crucial for the health and longevity of your business. This chapter will demystify the financial aspects of running an LLC and help you navigate the world of business taxes with confidence.

Sec. 4.1: The Basics of LLC Taxation

Understanding the basics of LLC taxation is crucial for compliance and financial planning. LLCs offer flexibility in taxation, which can be advantageous for business owners. One of the biggest advantages of an LLC is its tax flexibility. By default, LLCs are treated as "pass-through" entities, meaning the business itself isn't taxed. Instead, profits and losses pass through to the members, who report them on their personal tax returns. This setup helps avoid the double taxation that corporations can face.

This section will provide an overview of the fundamental tax considerations for LLCs.

Pass-Through Taxation:

The default tax status for LLCs is pass-through taxation.

Single-Member LLCs: Treated as "disregarded entities" for tax purposes. Profits and losses are reported on the owner's personal tax return (Schedule C of Form 1040).

Multi-Member LLCs: Treated as partnerships. Profits and losses are passed through to the members, who report them on their personal tax returns (Schedule K-1 of Form 1065).

Example: If GreenThumb Gardens LLC is a multi-member LLC, each member reports their share of the profits on their individual tax returns.

Electing Corporate Taxation:

LLCs can elect to be taxed as a corporation, either as a C corporation or an S corporation.

C Corporation: Profits are taxed at the corporate level, and dividends distributed to members are taxed again at the individual level (double taxation).

S Corporation: Profits and losses are passed through to members, similar to a partnership, but members can be paid salaries, potentially reducing self-employment taxes.

Example: GreenThumb Gardens LLC elects S corporation status to take advantage of potential tax savings on self-employment taxes.

Self-Employment Taxes:

Members of an LLC may be subject to self-employment taxes on their share of the profits.

Social Security and Medicare: Self-employment taxes cover Social Security and Medicare contributions.

Deductions: A portion of self-employment taxes can be deducted on the owner's personal tax return.

Example: Members of GreenThumb Gardens LLC pay self-employment taxes on their earnings but deduct half of the tax on their personal tax returns.

Employment Taxes:

If your LLC has employees, you are responsible for employment taxes.

Withholding: Withhold income taxes, Social Security, and Medicare from employees' paychecks.

Employer Contributions: Pay the employer's share of Social Security and Medicare taxes.

Unemployment Taxes: Pay federal and state unemployment taxes.

Example: GreenThumb Gardens LLC withholds the appropriate taxes from its employees' paychecks and pays the employer's share of payroll taxes.

Sales and Use Taxes:

If your LLC sells goods or services, you may need to collect and remit sales and use taxes.

Collection: Collect sales tax from customers at the point of sale.

Remittance: Remit the collected taxes to the state tax authority.

Example: GreenThumb Gardens LLC collects sales tax on its landscaping services and remits it to the state.

Conclusion:

The basics of LLC taxation involve understanding pass-through taxation, the option to elect corporate taxation, self-employment taxes, employment taxes, and sales and use taxes. Navigating these tax considerations is essential for legal compliance and can also provide opportunities for tax planning and savings.

Sec. 4.2: Choosing Your Tax Status

While the default tax status for LLCs is pass-through, you have options. If it's financially beneficial, you can elect to have your LLC taxed as a corporation (either C-Corp or S-Corp). **This decision can have significant tax implications, so it's wise to consult with a tax professional to determine the best choice for your business**. This section will guide you through the options and considerations for choosing your LLC's tax status.

Default Tax Status:

By default, the IRS taxes LLCs based on the number of members.

Single-Member LLCs: Automatically treated as a disregarded entity, meaning the LLC's income and expenses are reported on the owner's personal tax return.

Multi-Member LLCs: Automatically taxed as a partnership, with profits and losses passed through to the members, who report them on their personal tax returns.

Example: GreenThumb Gardens LLC, with two members, is automatically taxed as a partnership unless it elects otherwise.

Electing Corporate Taxation:

LLCs have the option to elect to be taxed as a corporation.

C Corporation (Form 8832): Electing C corporation status subjects the LLC to corporate income tax. Profits distributed as dividends are taxed again at the individual level.

S Corporation (Form 2553): Electing S corporation status allows profits and losses to pass through to members, similar to a partnership, but members can draw salaries as employees, potentially reducing self-employment taxes.

Example: GreenThumb Gardens LLC elects S corporation status to take advantage of payroll tax savings for its members.

Considerations for Choosing Tax Status:

Several factors should be considered when choosing your LLC's tax status.

Tax Liability: Compare the tax implications of each status, including self-employment taxes and potential double taxation as a C corporation.

Administrative Burden: Consider the administrative requirements, such as payroll processing for S corporations.

Future Plans: Think about your long-term business goals and how each tax status aligns with those plans.

Professional Advice: Consult with a tax professional to understand the implications of each option and make an informed decision.

Example: GreenThumb Gardens LLC consults with a CPA to analyze the tax implications of each status before making an election.

Changing Your Tax Status:

If your business needs change, you can change your LLC's tax status.

Revoking S Corporation Status: If you've elected S corporation status, you can revoke it with IRS consent.

Re-Electing S Corporation Status: There are restrictions on how often you can elect and revoke S corporation status.

Example: GreenThumb Gardens LLC initially elects S corporation status but later revokes it when the business structure changes.

Conclusion:

Choosing your LLC's tax status is a significant decision that can impact your tax liability and administrative responsibilities. By understanding the default tax treatment, the options for electing corporate taxation, and the considerations for making an informed choice, you can select the tax status that best aligns with your business objectives.

Sec. 4.3: Self-Employment Taxes

Self-employment taxes are a critical aspect of tax planning for LLC members. These taxes contribute to your Social Security and Medicare benefits and are based on the profits of your business. Understanding how self-employment taxes work can help you plan and save effectively. This section will delve into the details of self-employment taxes for LLC members.

Understanding Self-Employment Taxes:

Self-employment taxes consist of two parts:

Social Security Tax: A percentage of your profits goes towards your Social Security benefits, which provide retirement, disability, and survivor benefits.

Medicare Tax: A percentage of your profits contributes to Medicare, the health insurance program for people aged 65 and older, and some younger people with disabilities.

Calculating Self-Employment Taxes:

The self-employment tax rate is a combination of the Social Security and Medicare tax rates.

Total Rate: The total self-employment tax rate is 15.3%, comprising 12.4% for Social Security and 2.9% for Medicare.

Net Earnings: Self-employment taxes are calculated based on the net earnings of your LLC, which is the profit after deducting business expenses.

Example: If GreenThumb Gardens LLC has a net profit of $100,000, the self-employment tax would be $15,300 ($100,000 x 15.3%).

Deducting Self-Employment Taxes:

You can deduct a portion of your self-employment taxes when calculating your adjusted gross income.

Deduction: You can deduct the employer-equivalent portion of your self-employment tax, which is 50% of the total self-employment tax.

Example: If the self-employment tax for GreenThumb Gardens LLC is $15,300, the deduction would be $7,650.

Paying Self-Employment Taxes:

Self-employment taxes are typically paid through estimated tax payments.

Estimated Taxes: LLC members often need to make quarterly estimated tax payments to the IRS, which include both income tax and self-employment tax.

Form 1040-ES: Use Form 1040-ES to calculate and pay estimated taxes.

Example: Members of GreenThumb Gardens LLC make quarterly estimated tax payments based on their expected net earnings for the year.

Reducing Self-Employment Taxes:

There are strategies to potentially reduce self-employment taxes.

S Corporation Election: By electing S corporation status, LLC members can draw a reasonable salary and potentially reduce self-employment taxes on the remaining profits.

Business Expenses: Deducting legitimate business expenses reduces net earnings and, consequently, self-employment taxes.

Example: GreenThumb Gardens LLC elects S corporation status, and members draw a reasonable salary, reducing self-employment taxes on the remaining profits.

Conclusion:

Self-employment taxes are an essential consideration for LLC members. By understanding how these taxes are calculated, deducted, and paid, and exploring strategies to potentially reduce them, you can effectively manage your tax obligations and plan for your financial future.

Sec. 4.4: Quarterly Estimated Taxes

For many LLC members, paying taxes is not just an annual event but a quarterly one. This is due to the requirement to pay estimated taxes throughout the year. Understanding and managing these payments is crucial to avoid underpayment penalties and manage cash flow effectively. This section will explain the concept of quarterly estimated taxes and how to navigate them.

What Are Quarterly Estimated Taxes?

Quarterly estimated taxes are prepayments of the taxes you expect to owe for the year. They include both income tax and self-employment tax.

Who Pays Them: Typically, if you expect to owe at least $1,000 in taxes after subtracting withholdings and credits, you must make estimated tax payments.

Why They Exist: Since income from an LLC is not subject to tax withholding like a traditional salary, the IRS requires these payments to collect taxes as income is earned.

Calculating Estimated Taxes:

To calculate your estimated taxes, you'll need to estimate your adjusted gross income, taxable income, taxes, deductions, and credits for the year.

Form 1040-ES: The IRS provides Form 1040-ES, which includes a worksheet to help you estimate your taxes and calculate your quarterly payments.

Safe Harbor Rule: To avoid penalties, you must pay at least 90% of the tax you owe for the current year or 100% of the tax you owed for the previous year (110% if your adjusted gross income is more than $150,000).

Making Payments:

Estimated tax payments are due four times a year.

Deadlines: Payments are typically due on April 15, June 15, September 15, and January 15 (of the following year).

Payment Methods: You can pay online, by phone, or by mail using the vouchers included in Form 1040-ES.

Example:

GreenThumb Gardens LLC estimates its tax liability for the year to be $40,000. To avoid underpayment penalties, they decide to use the safe harbor rule and pay 100% of last year's tax liability, which was $36,000. They divide this amount by four and make quarterly payments of $9,000.

Adjusting Payments:

If your income changes significantly during the year, you may need to adjust your estimated payments.

Increased Income: If your income is higher than expected, you may need to increase your payments to avoid underpayment penalties.

Decreased Income: If your income is lower than expected, you may reduce your payments.

Record Keeping: The dispassionate advice is to get help from a professional accountant.

Keep detailed records of your estimated tax payments. You'll need to report them on your tax return at the end of the year.

Conclusion:

Quarterly estimated taxes are a critical part of tax management for LLC members. By understanding how to calculate, make, and adjust your payments, you can ensure compliance with IRS requirements and manage your business's cash flow effectively.

Sec. 4.5: Deductions and Credits

Navigating the world of deductions and credits can significantly impact the tax liability of an LLC. Understanding what expenses are deductible and what credits you may be eligible for can lead to substantial tax savings. This section will explore common deductions and credits available to LLCs and how to apply them effectively.

Understanding Deductions:

Deductions reduce your taxable income, which in turn, lowers your tax liability.

Ordinary and Necessary: The IRS allows you to deduct expenses that are considered both ordinary (common in your trade or business) and necessary (appropriate and helpful for your business).

Common Deductions: These can include rent, utilities, supplies, equipment, business travel, and salaries paid to employees.

Home Office Deduction: If you use part of your home regularly and exclusively for business, you may be able to deduct a portion of your housing expenses.

Example: GreenThumb Gardens LLC deducts expenses for gardening supplies, employee salaries, and a portion of the home office expenses.

Capitalizing vs. Deducting:

Some expenses must be capitalized rather than deducted, meaning they are added to the cost basis of an asset and depreciated over time.

Capital Expenditures: These are typically larger purchases like property or equipment that have a useful life beyond the current tax year.

Depreciation: This allows you to spread the cost of the asset over its useful life.

Example: GreenThumb Gardens LLC purchases a new truck for deliveries and capitalizes the expense, depreciating it over the truck's expected lifespan.

Understanding Credits:

Credits provide a dollar-for-dollar reduction in your tax liability and are generally more beneficial than deductions.

Common Credits: These can include the Small Business Health Care Tax Credit, the Work Opportunity Tax Credit, and the Disabled Access Credit.

Eligibility: Credits often have specific eligibility requirements, so it's important to understand the criteria for each credit you claim.

Example: GreenThumb Gardens LLC may be eligible for the Work Opportunity Tax Credit if they hire veterans or other qualifying individuals.

Record Keeping:

Maintaining accurate records is essential for substantiating your deductions and credits.

Receipts and Invoices: Keep all receipts and invoices related to business expenses.

Documentation: Maintain documentation for credits claimed, such as forms and certifications.

Example: GreenThumb Gardens LLC keeps detailed records of all business expenses and maintains forms for any tax credits claimed.

Conclusion:

Deductions and credits are powerful tools for reducing the tax liability of your LLC. By understanding what expenses are deductible, how to capitalize and depreciate assets, and what credits you may be eligible for, you can maximize your tax savings and reduce your overall tax burden.

Sec. 4.6: State and Local Taxes

While federal taxes often take center stage in tax planning, state and local taxes can also have a significant impact on your LLC's financial health. These taxes vary widely depending on where your LLC is located and operates. Understanding and managing these obligations is crucial for compliance and financial planning. This section will explore the various types of state and local taxes that may apply to your LLC.

State Income Taxes:

Many states impose an income tax on businesses, including LLCs.

Pass-Through Taxation: In states with income tax, LLC profits are often taxed at the member level, similar to federal taxes.

Franchise Taxes or Fees: Some states charge a franchise tax or fee for the privilege of doing business in the state.

Example: GreenThumb Gardens LLC, located in a state with income tax, reports its profits on the members' state tax returns and pays any applicable franchise fees.

Sales Taxes:

If your LLC sells goods or certain services, you may be required to collect and remit sales tax.

Registration: You must register with your state's taxing authority to collect sales tax.

Collection and Filing: Collect sales tax from customers and file regular sales tax returns with the state.

Example: GreenThumb Gardens LLC registers to collect sales tax on its gardening supplies and remits the collected taxes to the state.

Property Taxes:

If your LLC owns real property, you may be subject to property taxes.

Assessment: Property taxes are typically based on the assessed value of the property.

Local Rates: Rates and assessment methods vary by locality.

Example: GreenThumb Gardens LLC pays annual property taxes on its greenhouse and office space.

Payroll Taxes:

If your LLC has employees, you'll need to manage payroll taxes at the state and local level.

Withholding Taxes: Withhold state income tax from employees' wages, if applicable.

Unemployment Insurance: Pay state unemployment insurance taxes.

Example: GreenThumb Gardens LLC withholds state income tax from its employees' paychecks and pays into the state unemployment insurance fund.

Other Local Taxes:

Depending on your location, there may be additional local taxes, such as business license taxes, gross receipts taxes, or occupancy taxes.

Local Regulations: Check with your local government to understand any additional tax obligations.

Example: GreenThumb Gardens LLC pays an annual business license tax to the city where it operates.

Navigating Multi-State Operations:

If your LLC operates in multiple states, you may have tax obligations in each state.

Nexus: Establishing a business presence or "nexus" in a state can trigger tax obligations.

Apportionment: Profits may need to be apportioned among states based on various factors.

Example: GreenThumb Gardens LLC opens a second location in another state and must navigate the tax implications in both states.

Conclusion:

State and local taxes are a complex but essential part of managing your LLC. By understanding the types of taxes that may apply, registering and filing appropriately, and staying informed about the tax landscape in your area, you can ensure compliance and optimize your tax strategy.

Sec. 4.7: Hiring a Tax Professional

Navigating the complexities of LLC taxation can be daunting, especially for beginners. While many small business owners manage their own taxes, there comes a point where the expertise of a tax professional can be invaluable. This section will discuss the benefits of hiring a tax professional and how to find the right one for your LLC.

Benefits of Hiring a Tax Professional:

Expertise: Tax professionals are well-versed in the intricacies of tax law and can help ensure you're compliant with all regulations.

Maximizing Deductions and Credits: They can help identify all the deductions and credits you're entitled to, potentially saving you significant money.

Time-Saving: Outsourcing tax preparation saves you time, allowing you to focus on running your business.

Audit Support: In the event of an audit, having a tax professional by your side can be reassuring and beneficial.

Strategic Planning: Tax professionals can assist with long-term tax planning, helping you make strategic decisions that minimize your tax liability.

Finding the Right Tax Professional:

Credentials: Look for a Certified Public Accountant (CPA), Enrolled Agent (EA), or a tax attorney, as they have the qualifications to handle complex tax issues.

Experience: Choose someone with experience in your industry and with LLCs specifically.

Reputation: Check reviews and ask for references to gauge the professional's reputation.

Availability: Ensure they are available to answer questions and provide assistance throughout the year, not just during tax season.

Fees: Understand their fee structure upfront to avoid surprises.

Working with Your Tax Professional:

Provide Records: Share all relevant financial records, receipts, and documents with your tax professional.

Be Transparent: Disclose all sources of income and potential deductions. Transparency is key to accurate tax preparation.

Ask Questions: Use the opportunity to learn from their expertise. Ask questions about your taxes and how different business decisions might impact them.

Review Filings: Before submitting any tax filings, review them carefully to ensure accuracy and understanding.

Example:

GreenThumb Gardens LLC decides to hire a CPA with experience in the gardening industry. The CPA helps them identify additional deductions, provides strategic advice on tax-efficient business practices, and assists with quarterly tax filings.

Conclusion:

Hiring a tax professional can provide peace of mind, save

money, and free up time for you to focus on your business. By choosing the right professional and working closely with them, you can navigate the complexities of LLC taxation with confidence.

Sec. 4.8: Keeping Accurate Records

For LLCs, maintaining accurate and comprehensive records is not just a good business practice—it's a legal requirement. Proper record-keeping supports the financial health of your business, ensures compliance with tax laws, and can protect your limited liability status. This section will delve into the importance of record-keeping and how to maintain your business records effectively.

Importance of Accurate Records:

Tax Preparation: Accurate records are essential for preparing your tax returns and supporting your deductions and credits.

Audit Trail: Should your LLC face an audit, well-kept records will provide the necessary documentation to support your tax filings.

Financial Analysis: Detailed records allow for better financial analysis and decision-making, helping you to understand the financial state of your business and plan for the future.

Legal Protection: Keeping proper records can help maintain your LLC's limited liability protection by demonstrating that the business is separate from its owners.

What Records to Keep:

Financial Statements: This includes balance sheets, income statements, cash flow statements, and statements of shareholders' equity.

Bank Statements: Retain all bank statements to reconcile with your books.

Receipts and Invoices: Keep all receipts and invoices related to business expenses to substantiate deductions.

Tax Returns: Keep copies of all filed tax returns and related documents.

Employment Records: If you have employees, maintain all payroll records and employment tax filings.

Legal Documents: Articles of Organization, Operating Agreement, licenses, permits, and any contracts or agreements.

Record-Keeping Best Practices:

Consistency: Use a consistent method for tracking and recording transactions.

Timeliness: Update records regularly to avoid a backlog of unrecorded transactions.

Digital Backups: Keep digital copies of important documents to prevent loss due to damage or disaster.

Retention Policy: Know the retention requirements for each type of record (typically, tax records should be kept for at least seven years).

Separation of Personal and Business: Always keep personal finances separate from business records to maintain clear boundaries.

Tools for Record-Keeping:

Accounting Software: Use accounting software like QuickBooks, Xero, or FreshBooks to streamline the record-keeping process.

Document Management Systems: Consider using a document management system to organize and store digital records.

Professional Help: Engage a bookkeeper or accountant for regular record maintenance and review.

Example:

GreenThumb Gardens LLC uses QuickBooks to manage its financial records, stores receipts digitally, and has a CPA review its records quarterly to ensure accuracy and compliance.

Conclusion:

Accurate record-keeping is a cornerstone of successful LLC management. By implementing a robust system for maintaining your records, you can ensure that your business operations are transparent, compliant, and prepared for any financial scrutiny.

Conclusion of Chapter 4:

Navigating taxes and managing money are critical skills for any LLC owner. By understanding your tax obligations, taking advantage of deductions and credits, and keeping accurate financial records, you can ensure your business remains financially sound and compliant with tax laws. In the next chapter, we'll explore the ongoing requirements to keep your LLC in good standing.

5. Chapter 5: Keeping Your LLC in Good Standing

Maintaining your LLC's good standing is crucial for the legitimacy and legal protection of your business. This chapter will guide you through the ongoing requirements and best practices to ensure your LLC remains compliant and in good standing with state and federal regulations.

Sec. 5.1: Annual Reports and Filings

One of the key responsibilities of maintaining an LLC is the submission of annual reports and other required filings. These documents are crucial for keeping your business in good standing with state and federal agencies. This section will guide you through the process of preparing and submitting these reports.

Understanding Annual Reports:

Purpose: Annual reports update the state on your LLC's activities, changes in membership, and confirm contact information.

Requirements: Most states require LLCs to file an annual report, also known as a statement of information or annual statement.

Deadlines: The due date varies by state but is often on the anniversary of the LLC's formation or the end of the fiscal year.

Information Typically Included:

Business Name and Address: Confirm or update the official name and primary location of your business.

Registered Agent: Verify or change the registered agent and their address.

Management Structure: Update any changes in management, such as new members or managers.

Business Activities: Describe the general nature of your business activities over the past year.

Preparing Your Annual Report:

Review State Requirements: Each state has different forms and specific information requirements for annual reports.

Gather Information: Compile all necessary information, including financial statements and records of any changes in the business.

Complete the Form: Fill out the annual report form provided by your state's business filing agency.

Filing Your Annual Report:

Filing Methods: Many states allow or require online filing, while others may accept mail submissions.

Fees: There is typically a filing fee, which varies by state.

Timeliness: Submit your report by the deadline to avoid late fees or penalties, which can include the dissolution of your LLC.

Other Required Filings:

Tax Filings: In addition to the annual report, your LLC must file the appropriate tax documents with the IRS and state tax agencies.

Special Permits and Licenses: Renew any permits or licenses required for your business operations.

Statement of Information: Some states require this document, which is similar to an annual report but may be due at different intervals.

Record Keeping:

Documentation: Keep copies of all filings and receipts confirming submission and payment of fees.

Calendar Alerts: Set reminders for upcoming deadlines to ensure timely compliance.

Example:

GreenThumb Gardens LLC reviews its records in preparation for the annual report. They update the business address, confirm the registered agent, and describe their expanded services. They file online and pay the required fee before the due date.

Conclusion:

Annual reports and other filings are not just bureaucratic paperwork; they are legal requirements that keep your LLC legitimate and operational. By understanding what is required and staying organized, you can ensure that these obligations are met, maintaining the good standing of your LLC.

Sec. 5.2: Renewing Business Licenses and Permits

Maintaining the legal operation of your LLC involves ensuring that all necessary business licenses and permits are up to date. These authorizations are typically issued by various government agencies and can range from general business licenses to specific permits for certain activities. This section will outline the steps for renewing these critical documents.

Understanding Business Licenses and Permits:

Variety of Licenses: Depending on your industry, location, and activities, your LLC may require multiple licenses and permits from local, state, and federal agencies.

Renewal Periods: Licenses and permits have expiration dates and must be renewed periodically to avoid fines or business interruption.

Staying Informed: It's essential to be aware of the specific renewal requirements for each license and permit your business holds.

Steps for Renewal:

Inventory of Licenses and Permits: Keep a list of all licenses and permits, including their expiration dates and renewal requirements.

Review Changes in Regulations: Regulations can change, so review any updates that might affect your renewal process or the conditions of your licenses.

Prepare Documentation: Gather all necessary documentation required for renewal, which may include proof of continued business operations, updated business information, and financial records.

Submit Renewal Applications: Complete and submit renewal applications before the expiration dates. Some agencies may offer grace periods, but it's best to renew early to avoid lapses.

Renewal Process:

Online Renewals: Many agencies now offer online renewal services, which can be more convenient and faster than traditional methods.

Fees: Be prepared to pay renewal fees, which will vary depending on the license or permit type.

Inspections: Some renewals may require inspections or additional certifications, so schedule these in advance to meet renewal deadlines.

Record Keeping:

Confirmation of Renewal: Keep confirmation receipts or certificates that prove your licenses and permits have been renewed.

Digital Copies: Store digital copies of all licenses and permits in a secure but accessible location.

Calendar Alerts: Set reminders for future renewal dates well in advance to ensure continuous compliance.

Example:

GreenThumb Gardens LLC operates with a general business license, a nursery license, and a pesticide application permit. As renewal dates approach, they

review any changes in agricultural regulations, submit renewal applications online, pay the necessary fees, and schedule a pesticide storage inspection required for the permit.

Conclusion:

Renewing business licenses and permits is a critical aspect of maintaining your LLC's legal compliance and operational status. By keeping organized records, staying informed about regulatory changes, and proactively managing renewals, you can ensure that your business operations remain uninterrupted and on the right side of the law.

Sec. 5.3: Complying with Tax Obligations

For LLCs, tax compliance is a critical aspect of legal and financial responsibility. It involves understanding and fulfilling all tax obligations at the federal, state, and local levels. This section will provide an overview of these obligations and offer guidance on how to comply with them effectively.

Understanding Tax Obligations:

Federal Taxes: LLCs are typically taxed as pass-through entities, meaning profits and losses are reported on the personal tax returns of the members. However, an LLC can elect to be taxed as a corporation if beneficial.

State Taxes: Depending on the state, an LLC may be subject to income taxes, franchise taxes, or other state-specific taxes.

Local Taxes: Some local jurisdictions may require additional taxes to be paid, such as property tax if the LLC owns real estate, or sales tax for products and services sold.

Steps for Tax Compliance:

Know Your Deadlines: Be aware of all tax filing deadlines to avoid penalties and interest for late submissions.

Maintain Good Records: Keep accurate and detailed financial records throughout the year to make tax preparation easier.

Understand Your Tax Responsibilities: Know which taxes your LLC is liable for and the appropriate forms needed for filing.

Make Estimated Tax Payments: If required, make quarterly estimated tax payments to the IRS and state tax authorities.

Filing Taxes:

Federal Tax Returns: File IRS Form 1040 Schedule C, E, or F for pass-through taxation, or Form 1120 if taxed as a corporation.

State Tax Returns: File the necessary state tax returns, which vary by state.

Local Tax Filings: Submit any required local tax filings, which may include sales tax returns or property tax statements.

Employment Taxes:

Payroll Taxes: If your LLC has employees, you must withhold the correct amount of payroll taxes and submit them to the

IRS.

Unemployment Taxes: Pay state unemployment taxes and file the required reports.

Sales Taxes:

Collection and Remittance: If applicable, collect sales tax from customers and remit it to the appropriate tax authority.

Use of Tax Professionals:

Consult Experts: Consider hiring a tax professional or accountant who can provide expert advice and ensure that your LLC complies with all tax obligations.

Audit Representation: A tax professional can also represent your LLC in the event of a tax audit.

Example:

GreenThumb Gardens LLC consults with a CPA to understand their tax obligations. They file their federal tax return using Schedule C and pay state franchise taxes. They also collect and remit sales tax for their product sales and file employment tax reports for their staff.

Conclusion:

Tax compliance is an ongoing process that requires attention to detail and an understanding of complex regulations. By staying informed, keeping accurate records, and seeking professional advice when necessary, your LLC can maintain good standing with tax authorities and avoid costly penalties.

Sec. 5.4: Updating Your Operating Agreement

An Operating Agreement is a foundational document for an LLC, outlining the ownership structure, member roles, and operational procedures. As your LLC grows and evolves, it's crucial to update this document to reflect changes in the business and ensure it continues to provide clear guidance for management and operations. This section will guide you through the considerations and processes for updating your Operating Agreement.

Understanding the Importance of an Updated Operating Agreement:

Reflects Current Operations: An up-to-date Operating Agreement ensures that the document accurately reflects how the LLC is currently run.

Clarifies Member Expectations: Changes in membership or management roles can be clearly defined and understood by all parties.

Legal Compliance: An updated Operating Agreement can help maintain limited liability protection by showing that the LLC is following proper procedures.

When to Update Your Operating Agreement:

Change in Membership: Adding or removing members, or changing the ownership percentages among members.

Management Adjustments: Changing from member-managed to manager-managed, or vice versa, or altering the responsibilities of members/managers.

Operational Changes: Modifying the scope of the business, decision-making processes, or other operational details.

Financial Revisions: Updating capital contributions, profit distribution methods, or financial management procedures.

Regulatory Compliance: Ensuring the agreement complies with new laws or regulations.

Steps for Updating Your Operating Agreement:

Review Current Agreement: Assess the existing Operating Agreement to determine which sections require updates.

Consult Members: Engage with all members to discuss proposed changes and reach a consensus.

Draft Amendments: Write clear and concise amendments to the Operating Agreement or draft a new agreement if substantial changes are needed.

Legal Review: Consider having the updated agreement reviewed by an attorney to ensure legal validity and compliance.

Member Approval: Obtain formal approval from all members, typically requiring a majority or unanimous vote, depending on the existing agreement's terms.

Execute Changes: Sign and date the updated Operating Agreement, with all members receiving a copy for their records.

File with State Agencies: If required by your state, file the updated Operating Agreement or amendments with the appropriate state agency.

Record Keeping:

Document Version Control: Keep a record of all versions of the Operating Agreement, including the dates of amendments.

Member Acknowledgment: Ensure that all members acknowledge the updates in writing, which can be important in the event of disputes.

Example:

GreenThumb Gardens LLC has expanded its operations to include landscaping services. The members agree to update their Operating Agreement to reflect the new business activities and to redefine the profit-sharing structure. They draft the amendments, have them reviewed by an attorney, and all members sign off on the changes.

Conclusion:

An Operating Agreement is a living document that should grow with your LLC. Regularly reviewing and updating it ensures that it remains relevant and effective in governing your LLC's operations. This proactive approach can prevent misunderstandings among members and ensure smooth business operations.

Sec. 5.5: Maintaining Accurate Records

Accurate record-keeping is not just a cornerstone of sound business management; it's also a legal requirement for LLCs. It helps in tracking the company's progress, supports financial decisions, and is crucial during tax season or legal inquiries. This section will provide guidance on how to maintain your LLC's records accurately.

Understanding the Need for Accurate Records:

Legal Compliance: Accurate records demonstrate that the LLC is operating according to its stated structure and complies with relevant laws.

Financial Integrity: They provide a true representation of the LLC's financial health and are essential for reporting to investors or financial institutions.

Audit Preparedness: In the event of an audit, well-maintained records can expedite the process and potentially avoid penalties.

Types of Records to Maintain:

Financial Documents: This includes bank statements, receipts, invoices, payroll records, and ledgers detailing income and expenses.

Meeting Minutes: Records of meetings, especially those that involve major decisions or changes in the LLC, should be documented and stored.

Legal Documents: The Articles of Organization, Operating Agreement, amendments, and any contracts or legal agreements must be kept up to date.

Tax Records: All tax returns and related documents should be retained for at least seven years, as recommended by the IRS.

Licenses and Permits: Copies of current business licenses, permits, and related renewal documents.

Best Practices for Record Maintenance:

Regular Updates: Ensure that records are updated in real-time or on a regular schedule to avoid discrepancies.

Organized Storage: Keep records organized in a logical manner, whether in physical files or digital format, for easy retrieval.

Secure Backup: Implement a system for backing up records, ideally in multiple locations or using cloud storage services.

Access Control: Limit access to sensitive records to authorized personnel to maintain confidentiality and integrity.

Review and Audit: Periodically review records for accuracy and completeness, and conduct internal audits if necessary.

Digital Record-Keeping:

Accounting Software: Utilize accounting software to automate financial record-keeping and ensure accuracy.

Document Management Systems: Employ document management systems to organize and secure digital records.

Digital Security: Ensure that digital records are protected with appropriate cybersecurity measures.

Example:

GreenThumb Gardens LLC uses a cloud-based accounting system to manage its financial records. They hold quarterly meetings to review financial reports, and minutes are recorded and stored in a secure online repository. They also have a digital folder for all legal documents, which is backed up regularly.

Conclusion:

Maintaining accurate records is a continuous process that requires diligence and organization. By employing the right tools and practices, your LLC can ensure that its records are always up-to-date, secure, and compliant with legal standards. This not only protects the LLC but also provides a solid foundation for making informed business decisions.

Sec. 5.6: Complying with Employment Laws

For LLCs with employees, compliance with employment laws is an important aspect of operations. These laws cover a wide range of areas including wages, workplace safety, anti-discrimination practices, and benefits. This section will help you understand the basics of employment law compliance for your LLC.

Understanding Employment Laws:

Fair Labor Standards Act (FLSA): This act sets the standards for minimum wage, eligibility for overtime pay, guidelines for recordkeeping, and regulations for employing minors.

Occupational Safety and Health Act (OSHA): Mandates that employers maintain a workplace environment that is safe and healthy for their employees.

Equal Employment Opportunity (EEO) Laws: Prohibit discrimination against employees or job applicants based on race, color, religion, sex, national origin, age, disability, or genetic information.

Family and Medical Leave Act (FMLA): Provides eligible employees with unpaid, job-protected leave for specified family and medical reasons.

Steps for Compliance:

Educate Yourself and Management: Ensure that you and your management team are aware of all relevant employment laws.

Develop Policies and Procedures: Create clear workplace policies that comply with these laws, including anti-discrimination policies, safety protocols, and wage and hour rules.

Train Your Employees: Provide training to your employees on these policies to ensure understanding and compliance.

Keep Accurate Records: Maintain detailed records of employee hours, wages, and any incidents to ensure compliance with FLSA and OSHA requirements.

Post Required Notices: Display all required labor law posters in a conspicuous place where all employees can see them.

Handling Employment Taxes:

Withhold and Pay Taxes: Withhold the correct amount of federal, state, and local taxes from employees' paychecks and make the necessary payments to tax agencies.

File Employment Tax Reports: Submit the required reports to the IRS and state tax agencies on a quarterly and annual basis.

Managing Employee Benefits:

Understand Benefit Requirements: Determine which benefits are required by law for your employees, such as workers' compensation insurance.

Offer and Manage Benefits: If you offer additional benefits like health insurance or retirement plans, ensure they are managed in compliance with applicable laws.

Staying Updated:

Monitor Legal Changes: Employment laws can change, so it's important to stay informed about any updates or new laws that may affect your LLC.

Consult with Professionals: Consider working with a human resources professional or employment lawyer to ensure ongoing compliance.

Example:

GreenThumb Gardens LLC conducts an annual review of its

employment practices. They update their employee handbook to reflect the latest labor laws, provide training sessions on workplace safety, and ensure their payroll system accurately tracks hours and wages.

Conclusion:

Compliance with employment laws is not only a legal requirement but also a best practice for creating a fair and safe work environment. By taking proactive steps to educate, develop policies, and maintain records, your LLC can minimize the risk of legal issues and create a positive workplace culture.

Sec. 5.7: Protecting Your Limited Liability Status

One of the primary reasons entrepreneurs choose the LLC structure is for the limited liability protection it offers. This protection can shield your personal assets from business debts and legal judgments. However, maintaining this protection requires careful adherence to certain practices and legal formalities. This section will guide you through the necessary steps to protect your LLC's limited liability status.

Understanding Limited Liability:

Separation of Assets: There must be a clear distinction between personal and business assets.

Adherence to Corporate Formalities: Even though an LLC has

more flexibility than a corporation, it still needs to follow certain formalities to maintain its status.

Proper Representation: The LLC should always be represented as a separate legal entity in all business activities and documents.

Steps to Protect Your Limited Liability:

Maintain Separate Finances: Do not commingle personal funds with business funds. This includes having separate bank accounts and credit cards for the business.

Sign Documents Correctly: Always sign business documents in your capacity as a member or manager of the LLC, not personally.

Follow Your Operating Agreement: Adhere to the rules and procedures outlined in your LLC's Operating Agreement.

Keep Good Records: Document all business decisions and maintain accurate financial records.

Stay Compliant with Laws: Ensure that your business complies with all relevant laws and regulations, including tax obligations and employment laws.

Obtain Adequate Insurance: Protect your business with liability insurance to cover potential business liabilities.

Avoiding Actions That Can Jeopardize Protection:

Avoid Personal Guarantees: If possible, refrain from personally guaranteeing business loans or leases.

Do Not Engage in Fraudulent Activities: Engaging in illegal activities can pierce the corporate veil and expose members to personal liability.

Prevent Undercapitalization: Ensure your LLC is adequately funded to cover its operations and liabilities.

Regular Compliance Checks:

Annual Reviews: Conduct annual reviews of your business practices to ensure ongoing compliance with necessary formalities.

Update Documents as Needed: Amend your Operating Agreement and other legal documents as your business evolves.

Example:

GreenThumb Gardens LLC conducts an annual legal audit to ensure they are not inadvertently blurring the lines between personal and business activities. They update their Operating Agreement to reflect any changes in the business and invest in additional insurance coverage as they expand their services.

Conclusion:

Protecting your LLC's limited liability status is an ongoing process that requires diligent management and adherence to legal formalities. By taking proactive measures to separate personal and business affairs, maintain proper records, and comply with laws, you can safeguard the personal assets of the members and uphold the integrity of the LLC structure.

Sec. 5.8: Monitoring Changes in Laws and Regulations

Staying abreast of changes in laws and regulations is essential for any LLC. Legal landscapes evolve, and new regulations or amendments to existing laws can significantly impact your business operations. This section will outline strategies to ensure your LLC remains compliant with the latest legal requirements.

Understanding the Impact of Legal Changes:

Compliance: New laws may impose additional compliance requirements or alter existing ones.

Liability: Ignorance of the law is not a defense; failure to comply can result in fines, penalties, or legal action.

Competitive Advantage: Being aware of regulatory changes can provide strategic advantages, allowing for timely adaptation to new market conditions.

Strategies for Monitoring Legal Changes:

Government Resources: Utilize government websites and subscribe to newsletters from relevant regulatory agencies.

Legal Counsel: Establish a relationship with a legal advisor who can alert you to important changes affecting your industry.

Professional Associations: Join industry or trade associations that provide members with updates on laws and regulations.

Continuing Education: Attend seminars, webinars, and conferences focused on legal and regulatory issues in your field.

Compliance Software: Consider investing in compliance management software that tracks legal changes relevant to your business.

Implementing Changes in Your Business:

Review and Update Policies: Regularly review your business policies and procedures to ensure they align with current laws.

Train Your Team: Educate your employees about legal changes that affect their work and ensure they understand new compliance procedures.

Document Changes: Keep a record of how and when you updated your practices in response to changes in the law.

Staying Proactive:

Risk Assessment: Periodically conduct a risk assessment to identify areas where legal changes could impact your business.

Action Plan: Develop a plan for how your business will respond to significant legal changes, including budgeting for potential costs.

Regular Audits: Schedule regular audits to ensure your business is following all current laws and regulations.

Example:

GreenThumb Gardens LLC subscribes to a regulatory update

service that alerts them to changes in environmental and employment laws. They hold bi-annual training sessions for their staff to cover new compliance procedures and have a system in place to quickly update their Operating Agreement and other internal documents when necessary.

Conclusion:

Active monitoring of legal changes is a critical component of maintaining a compliant and successful LLC. By leveraging resources, seeking professional advice, and implementing a system for ongoing education and policy updates, your LLC can navigate the complexities of the legal environment and mitigate the risks associated with non-compliance.

Conclusion of Chapter 5:

Keeping your LLC in good standing is an ongoing process that requires attention to detail and a proactive approach. By fulfilling your reporting obligations, staying compliant with laws and regulations, and maintaining accurate records, you can protect your business and its reputation. In the next chapter, we'll discuss the considerations and steps involved if you ever decide to close your LLC.

6. Chapter 6: If You Decide to Close

There may come a time when you decide to close your LLC, whether it's due to retirement, a shift in business direction, or other personal reasons. This chapter will guide you through the process of dissolving your LLC properly and responsibly.

Sec. 6.1: Making the Decision to Dissolve

Deciding to dissolve an LLC is a significant step that requires careful consideration. This decision can be driven by various factors, such as changes in the market, personal circumstances of the members, or the financial health of the company. This section will guide you through the key considerations and the process involved in making the decision to dissolve your LLC.

Understanding the Reasons for Dissolution:

Business Goals Achieved: The LLC was formed for a specific purpose, and that purpose has been fulfilled.

Financial Challenges: The LLC is no longer financially viable, with debts outweighing profits.

Member Disagreements: Irreconcilable differences among members make it impossible to continue.

Market Changes: Shifts in the market or industry make the business model unsustainable.

Personal Reasons: Members may wish to retire or pursue other interests.

Key Considerations Before Dissolving:

Review the Operating Agreement: Check your LLC's Operating Agreement for any clauses related to dissolution and the required process.

Evaluate Financial Obligations: Assess all debts, liabilities, and ongoing contracts to understand the financial implications of dissolution.

Consider Alternatives: Explore all other options, such as selling the business or restructuring, before deciding on dissolution.

Member Vote: Typically, a formal vote by the LLC members is required to approve the dissolution.

Steps in the Decision-Making Process:

Hold a Meeting: Call a meeting with all members to discuss the potential dissolution and its implications.

Vote on Dissolution: Conduct a formal vote as stipulated by your Operating Agreement.

Document the Decision: If the decision to dissolve is made, document it in the form of a resolution or written consent.

Communicate with Stakeholders: Notify employees, customers, creditors, and other stakeholders of the decision.

Legal and Financial Implications:

Tax Considerations: Understand the tax consequences of

dissolution, including final tax returns.

Settling Debts: Create a plan for paying off debts and obligations.

Asset Distribution: Determine how remaining assets will be distributed among members after creditors are paid.

Example:

GreenThumb Gardens LLC has seen a steady decline in business due to a surge in competition. After reviewing their financials and considering market forecasts, the members hold a meeting and unanimously vote to dissolve the LLC. They document the decision and begin the process of notifying stakeholders and settling the company's affairs.

Conclusion:

Dissolution is a complex process that marks the end of your LLC's business activities. It should be approached with a full understanding of the legal, financial, and emotional ramifications. Careful planning, clear communication, and adherence to legal requirements will ensure the process is as smooth as possible. Our invitation is to have an experienced accountant assist you to avoid any repercussions.

Sec. 6.2: Filing Articles of Dissolution

Once the decision to dissolve an LLC has been made and properly documented, the next legal step is to file the Articles of Dissolution (sometimes known as the Certificate of Termination or Certificate of Dissolution) with the appropriate state agency, usually the Secretary of State's office. This formal document officially starts the process of ending the LLC's existence. Here's what you need to know about filing the Articles of Dissolution.

Understanding Articles of Dissolution:

Purpose: The Articles of Dissolution serve as a formal notice to the state that the LLC is ceasing operations and is winding up its affairs.

Information Required: Typically, the Articles of Dissolution will require the LLC's name, the date of dissolution, a statement that the decision to dissolve was properly made, and any other information required by state law.

State-Specific Forms: Each state has its own form and process for dissolution, so it's important to obtain and complete the correct form for your state.

Steps for Filing Articles of Dissolution:

Obtain the Form: Contact your state's Secretary of State office or visit their website to obtain the correct form.

Complete the Form: Fill out the form according to the instructions, providing all required information.

File with the State: Submit the completed form to the state agency, along with any required filing fee.

Receive Confirmation: The state will process the Articles of

Dissolution and send a confirmation that the LLC has been officially dissolved.

Legal Considerations:

Timing: Some states require that all debts and liabilities be settled before filing, while others allow for debts to be settled after filing.

Tax Clearance: Some states may require a tax clearance before processing the dissolution, confirming that all state taxes have been paid.

Notice to Creditors: Filing the Articles of Dissolution often triggers the requirement to formally notify creditors of the dissolution.

Financial Implications:

Final Taxes: Filing the Articles of Dissolution is a key step before filing final tax returns for the LLC.

Settling Debts: The LLC must settle or make plans to settle any outstanding debts.

Asset Distribution: After creditors are paid, any remaining assets can be distributed to the members according to the Operating Agreement or state law.

Example:

After GreenThumb Gardens LLC voted to dissolve, they obtained the Articles of Dissolution form from their state's website. The members completed the form, ensuring all information was accurate and reflective of their Operating Agreement. They filed the form with the state and paid the necessary fee. They received a confirmation of dissolution, which allowed them to move forward with notifying creditors and settling the company's financial obligations.

Conclusion:

Filing the Articles of Dissolution is a critical legal step in ending your LLC's business activities. It's important to follow your state's specific requirements and procedures to ensure a smooth and compliant dissolution process. Once filed, the LLC can proceed with winding up affairs, including notifying creditors, settling debts, and distributing any remaining assets.

Sec. 6.3: Notifying Creditors and Settling Debts

After filing the Articles of Dissolution, an LLC must take the necessary steps to notify its creditors and settle all outstanding debts. This process is crucial to avoid legal complications and to ensure that the members' liability remains limited. Here's a detailed guide on how to properly notify creditors and settle the LLC's debts.

Understanding the Process:

Legal Requirement: Notifying creditors is a legal requirement in the dissolution process and helps protect the LLC members from future claims.

Inventory of Obligations: Create a comprehensive list of all the LLC's debts and obligations, including loans, contracts, and accounts payable.

Steps for Notifying Creditors:

Identify Creditors: Compile a list of all known creditors, including any contingent liabilities.

Formal Notice: Send a formal written notice to each creditor, informing them of the LLC's dissolution and providing instructions for submitting claims.

Public Notice: Some states require a public notice of dissolution to be published in a newspaper, which informs potential claimants who might not be known to the LLC.

Claims Process: Establish a deadline for creditors to submit claims and a process for reviewing and approving or rejecting those claims.

Dispute Resolution: Be prepared to resolve disputes if creditors challenge the rejection of their claims.

Settling Debts:

Prioritize Claims: Follow state law to prioritize creditor claims, typically paying tax authorities first, followed by secured and unsecured creditors.

Payment Plan: If the LLC does not have enough assets to pay all claims at once, negotiate payment plans or settlements with creditors.

Final Payment: Make final payments to creditors, ensuring that receipts and releases are obtained to document the satisfaction of each debt.

Legal and Financial Considerations:

Limited Liability Protection: Properly notifying creditors and settling debts is essential to maintain the limited liability protection of the LLC members.

Insolvency: If the LLC is insolvent, consider consulting with a bankruptcy attorney to manage the process of paying creditors.

Remaining Assets: Only after all creditors' claims have been satisfied can any remaining assets be distributed to the LLC members.

Example:

GreenThumb Gardens LLC sends out notices to all their known creditors, including their suppliers and the bank that holds their business loan. They also publish a notice in the local newspaper to alert any unknown creditors. They review all claims received by the deadline and pay them in the order prescribed by law, using the remaining business assets. They negotiate a settlement with a creditor for a disputed claim to avoid protracted legal proceedings.

Conclusion:

Notifying creditors and settling debts is a critical step in the dissolution process that must be handled with diligence and transparency. It involves legal obligations that, if not properly managed, can lead to personal liability for LLC members. By following the correct procedures, the LLC can ensure that all debts are settled in a manner that is fair to creditors and safe for the LLC members.

Sec. 6.4: Liquidating Assets

Liquidating assets is a critical step in the dissolution process of an LLC. It involves converting the company's assets into cash to pay off debts, fulfill obligations to creditors, and distribute any remaining value to the members. This section will guide you through the process of asset liquidation.

Understanding Asset Liquidation:

Asset Inventory: Begin by creating a detailed inventory of all the LLC's assets, including physical property, intellectual property, and financial assets.

Valuation: Appraise the value of the assets to determine a fair market price for each item.

Sales Strategy: Develop a strategy for selling the assets, which may include private sales, auctions, or hiring a liquidation company.

Steps for Liquidating Assets:

Prioritize Liquidation: Determine the order in which assets will be sold, often starting with the easiest to convert to cash.

Sell Assets: Execute the sales strategy, ensuring that each transaction is properly documented with sales agreements and receipts.

Settle Secured Debts: Use the proceeds to pay off secured debts, as these creditors have a claim to specific assets.

Distribute Remaining Funds: After all debts and obligations are settled, distribute any remaining funds to the LLC members according to their ownership interests.

Legal and Financial Considerations:

Secured vs. Unsecured Creditors: Secured creditors have priority over specific assets, while unsecured creditors do not.

Fair Market Value: Assets should be sold for their fair market value to avoid claims of fraudulent transfer.

Tax Implications: Be aware of potential tax implications from the sale of assets, including capital gains tax.

Example:

GreenThumb Gardens LLC hires an appraiser to value their landscaping equipment, office furniture, and company vehicles. They decide to auction off the equipment and vehicles and sell the furniture to a neighboring business. The proceeds from these sales are used to pay off the company's secured business loan and outstanding invoices to suppliers. After all debts are paid, the remaining funds are distributed to the members.

Conclusion:

Liquidating assets is a process that must be approached methodically to ensure that the LLC's debts are paid and that members receive any remaining value. Proper documentation, adherence to legal priorities, and consideration of tax implications are all essential to a successful liquidation process.

Sec. 6.5: Handling Final Tax Obligations

As an LLC approaches dissolution, one of the final and most crucial steps is to handle all tax obligations. This ensures that the LLC is in good standing with tax authorities and prevents future tax liabilities for its members. This section will guide you through the process of fulfilling final tax duties.

Understanding Final Tax Obligations:

Final Returns: The LLC must file a final income tax return with the IRS and state tax authorities.

Employment Taxes: If the LLC has employees, it must settle any remaining employment tax responsibilities.

Capital Gains: The sale of assets during liquidation may result in capital gains taxes that need to be reported and paid.

Cancellations of Debt: If any debt is forgiven or canceled as part of the dissolution, there may be tax implications.

Steps for Handling Final Taxes:

Consult a Tax Professional: Consider hiring a tax advisor to ensure compliance with all tax laws and to take advantage of any available tax benefits.

File Final Federal Tax Return: Complete and file the final Form 1065 for partnerships or Form 1120 for LLCs taxed as corporations, and check the "final return" box.

Issue Final K-1 Forms: Provide members with their final Schedule K-1 forms, which report their share of the LLC's income and losses.

State Taxes: File any required state or local tax returns, and pay any outstanding state taxes.

Close Accounts: Notify the IRS and state tax agencies to close your business account and cancel your Employer Identification Number (EIN).

Legal and Financial Considerations:

Tax Clearance: Some states require a tax clearance before finalizing the dissolution, confirming that all state taxes have been paid.

Record-Keeping: Keep detailed records of all tax filings and payments in case of future audits or inquiries.

Debt Obligations: Ensure that all tax debts are settled to avoid personal liability for the LLC's members.

Example:

GreenThumb Gardens LLC works with their accountant to file their final federal tax return, indicating that it is the final return for the business. They also file final state tax returns and pay any remaining taxes due. After distributing the remaining assets to the members, the accountant issues final K-1 forms. Once all tax obligations are settled, they send a letter to the IRS to close their business tax account and cancel their EIN.

Conclusion:

Handling final tax obligations is a critical step in the dissolution process. It requires careful attention to detail and compliance with both federal and state tax laws. By ensuring all tax responsibilities are met, the LLC can avoid future liabilities and complete the dissolution process cleanly.

Sec. 6.6: Distributing Remaining Assets

After all debts, liabilities, and tax obligations have been settled, the final step in the dissolution process of an LLC is to distribute any remaining assets to the members. This process must be handled with care to ensure that it is done fairly and in accordance with the LLC's operating agreement and state laws.

Understanding Asset Distribution:

Member Interests: The distribution of remaining assets should reflect each member's ownership interest or the distribution provisions outlined in the LLC's operating agreement.

Asset Valuation: Remaining assets should be valued accurately to ensure that each member receives an equitable share.

Distribution Plan: Create a clear plan for how assets will be distributed, whether in the form of cash, property, or other assets.

Steps for Distributing Assets:

Review Operating Agreement: Refer to the LLC's operating agreement for guidance on how distributions should be made.

Determine Distribution Amounts: Calculate the amount each member is entitled to receive based on their ownership percentage or the terms of the operating agreement.

Liquidate Assets if Necessary: If the remaining assets are not in cash form, liquidate them to facilitate distribution.

Make Distributions: Distribute the assets to members, providing a clear statement of what is being distributed and the value of each distribution.

Obtain Receipts: Have each member acknowledge receipt of their distribution, which can help prevent disputes later on.

Legal and Financial Considerations:

Capital Accounts: Consider each member's capital account balance when determining distributions.

Tax Implications: Members may have tax obligations resulting from the distribution, such as capital gains tax.

Final Accounting: Perform a final accounting of the LLC's finances to accompany the distributions.

Example:

GreenThumb Gardens LLC has $50,000 in remaining assets

after paying all obligations. The operating agreement states that distributions are to be made based on ownership interest. John, who owns 60%, receives $30,000, and Susan, who owns 40%, receives $20,000. They both sign receipts acknowledging the distribution and are informed of potential tax implications.

Conclusion:

Distributing the remaining assets is the final act in the lifecycle of an LLC. It must be done with transparency and fairness, respecting the terms of the operating agreement and the ownership interests of the members. Proper documentation and clear communication can help ensure that this process concludes the LLC's affairs smoothly and without dispute.

Sec. 6.7: Keeping Records

Even after an LLC is dissolved, it is important to maintain records of its existence and operations. This is not only a legal requirement in many jurisdictions but also a practical measure to protect the former members from future liabilities or claims. Here's how to manage record-keeping after dissolution:

Understanding the Importance of Record-Keeping:

Legal Compliance: Many states require that business records be kept for a certain number of years after dissolution.

Audit Protection: Proper records can protect former members in the event of an audit or legal action.

Historical Reference: Records serve as a historical account of the business's operations and financial dealings.

Steps for Keeping Records:

Identify Required Records: Determine which records need to be retained, which typically include tax returns, financial statements, contracts, corporate minutes, and the operating agreement.

Choose a Storage Method: Decide on a method for storing records, whether in digital format, physical copies, or both.

Secure Storage: Ensure that the chosen storage method is secure and protected from theft, loss, or damage.

Designate a Custodian: Assign a responsible party to manage and maintain the records.

Communicate with Members: Inform all former members where and how records are stored and how they can be accessed if needed.

Legal and Financial Considerations:

Retention Period: Check state laws for the required retention period, which is commonly seven years but can vary.

Confidentiality: Maintain the confidentiality of sensitive information contained in the records.

Destruction Policy: Establish a policy for the eventual destruction of records once the retention period has expired, ensuring that it is done securely.

Example:

After the dissolution of GreenThumb Gardens LLC, the members decide to keep their records for the required seven-year period. They scan all important documents and store them on encrypted hard drives, which are kept in a fireproof safe. John is designated as the custodian of the records. They also keep physical copies in a secure storage facility. All members are provided with instructions on how to access these records if necessary.

Conclusion:

Keeping records after the dissolution of an LLC is a critical step that should not be overlooked. It requires careful planning and consideration of legal requirements. By ensuring that records are kept securely and can be accessed when needed, former members can protect themselves from future liabilities.

Sec. 6.8: Understanding the Emotional Impact

Dissolving an LLC is not only a legal and financial process but also an emotional journey for the members involved. Recognizing and managing the emotional impact is crucial for personal well-being and for maintaining professional relationships post-dissolution. Here's a guide to understanding and coping with the emotional side of dissolving an LLC.

Recognizing the Emotional Stages:

Acceptance: Coming to terms with the decision to dissolve can be challenging. Acceptance is the first step in moving forward.

Grief: Members may experience a sense of loss, similar to grief, as they let go of their business and the hopes and dreams associated with it.

Stress: The dissolution process can be stressful, with numerous tasks to complete and legal obligations to fulfill.

Relief: After the process is completed, members often feel a sense of relief, especially if the business was struggling.

Steps for Managing Emotions:

Open Communication: Encourage open and honest communication among members about their feelings and concerns.

Support System: Lean on a support system of family, friends, or professionals who can provide guidance and emotional support.

Professional Help: Consider seeking help from a counselor or therapist, especially if the dissolution is causing significant distress.

Reflect on Learnings: Take time to reflect on the experiences and lessons learned from running the LLC.

Plan for the Future: Focus on the future and new

opportunities, which can be a positive way to channel energy and emotions.

Legal and Financial Considerations:

Professional Demeanor: Despite the emotional toll, maintain professionalism throughout the dissolution process to ensure all legal and financial matters are handled appropriately.

Member Agreements: Be mindful of any emotional tensions that may affect negotiations or agreements among members.

Succession Planning: If the dissolution is part of a succession plan, managing emotions can be crucial for a smooth transition.

Example:

The members of GreenThumb Gardens LLC experience a mix of emotions during the dissolution process. They hold regular meetings to discuss not only the logistics but also how they are feeling about the end of their business venture. They agree to seek mediation to resolve any disputes amicably and decide to have a closing ceremony to mark the end of their journey and celebrate their achievements.

Conclusion:

The emotional impact of dissolving an LLC is significant and often overlooked. Acknowledging and addressing these emotions is essential for the well-being of the members and the smooth completion of the dissolution process. By taking proactive steps to manage emotions, members can close one chapter and move on to the next with a sense of closure and optimism.

Conclusion of Chapter 6:

Dissolving an LLC is a structured process that requires careful attention to legal and financial responsibilities. By following the proper steps and ensuring that all obligations are met, you can close your LLC with confidence and integrity. While it's the end of a chapter, it's also an opportunity for a new beginning.

Conclusion: A Word of Thanks

As we close the final pages of this guide, we would like to express our heartfelt gratitude to you, our readers. You began this journey with a desire to navigate the complexities of forming, managing, and maintaining an LLC, and we've been honored to serve as your compass.

Throughout this manual, we've tried to present the intricacies of LLCs in a manner that is not only simple and friendly, but also caring and professional. We hope the chapters have unfolded like a conversation with a trusted mentor, guiding you through each step with clarity and ease.

Your entrepreneurial spirit is the backbone of innovation and progress, and it's been our privilege to help you lay the groundwork for your business endeavors. We trust that the knowledge you've gained here will serve as a strong foundation for your future success.

If our words have illuminated the path to forming and maintaining your LLC, then we have fulfilled our mission. May the lessons contained in these pages enable you to move forward with confidence and assurance.

Thank you for allowing us to be a part of your entrepreneurial journey. We wish you all the best as you continue to grow and thrive in the business world. May your LLC not only succeed, but thrive in the years to come.

Sincerely and with best wishes,

Arnold Kent Tyler

Disclaimer

This manual is provided for educational purposes only and is designed to offer general information regarding the subject matter covered. It is not intended to provide legal, accounting, or other professional advice. While every effort has been made to ensure the accuracy and completeness of the information contained within this book, the author and publisher assume no responsibility for errors, omissions, or any changes in the laws and industry regulations that may have occurred before or after the publication of this manual.

The reader assumes full responsibility for their own decisions and actions regarding the topics covered in this book. The author and publisher disclaim any direct or indirect liability that may result from the use of the information contained herein.

It is strongly recommended that readers consult with a professional accountant or legal advisor before setting up and operating a Limited Liability Company (LLC). The guidance provided in this manual should not be considered as a substitute for personalized advice from a qualified professional.

Bonus

Scanning this QR code, or typing in the link below, will give you immediate access to the two promised bonuses:

1. the introductory video
2. the complete audio guide covering the entire book.

https://www.quickeasylearning.com/llc_beginners_guide/

If you are satisfied with this book, please consider leaving a review on the site where you made your purchase. Your feedback will help us grow and enhance our services. Both I and the broader community will be deeply grateful, and this gratitude will, in turn, aid in your own growth and improvement. Thank you.

Arnold Kent Tyler

www.ingramcontent.com/pod-product-compliance
Lightning Source LLC
Chambersburg PA
CBHW070018300526
45794CB00001B/356